ETHICAL DECISION MAKING
AND
INFORMATION TECHNOLOGY

ABOUT THE AUTHORS

Ernest A. Kallman is Professor of Computer Information Systems at Bentley College and a Research Fellow at the Bentley Center for Business Ethics. He coordinates the MIS course and also teaches systems analysis and design, I/S management, and I/S policy. Ernie holds a B.S. degree in Economics from St. Peters College, an M.B.A. from Baruch College, and a Ph.D. in Management Planning Systems from the City University of New York. Prior to entering academia he spent twelve years in the computer industry, where, among other positions, he was an officer and director of a software firm and a director of a mini-computer company.

Ernie has authored three books and numerous articles about the management of the information systems function, recently concentrating on ethical issues and privacy concerns. He is currently conducting a major research project on how organizations protect confidential information. He is also a consultant to organizations seeking to develop privacy policies and ethics training programs. At Bentley he is on a college-wide task force responsible for fostering ethics education across the curriculum.

John P. Grillo is Professor of Computer Information Systems at Bentley College and a Research Fellow at the Bentley Center for Business Ethics. He is coordinator of the introductory computer course and the department's Security and Privacy course, a popular elective offered at both the undergraduate and graduate levels.

At the University of New Mexico, John earned a Ph.D. in Educational Research, majoring in Computer Science. Before joining Bentley in 1979, he taught at the University of New Mexico, West Texas State University, and Western Illinois University.

John has co-authored (with J. D. Robertson, also of Bentley) fourteen texts and professional books in the areas of personal computer programming, graphics, and data structures. His present specialty is computer security and privacy, which initiated his interest in ethics.

ETHICAL DECISION MAKING AND INFORMATION TECHNOLOGY
An Introduction with Cases

Ernest A. Kallman
Bentley College

John P. Grillo
Bentley College

 Mitchell McGRAW-HILL
New York St. Louis San Francisco Auckland Bogotá Caracas
Lisbon London Madrid Mexico Milan Montreal New Delhi Paris
San Juan Singapore Sydney Tokyo Toronto Watsonville

To our wives, for their love and support . . .
Sandy and Betsy

Mitchell **McGRAW-HILL**
Watsonville, CA 95076

Ethical Decision Making and Information Technology
An Introduction with Cases

1 2 3 4 5 6 7 8 9 0 DOH DOH 9 0 9 8 7 6 5 4 3 2

ISBN 0–07–033884–1

Sponsoring editor: *Erika Berg*
Editorial assistant: *Jennifer Gilliland*
Director of production: *Jane Somers*
Production assistant: *Richard DeVitto*
Project manager: *Michael Bass & Associates*
Interior designer: *John Edeen*
Cover designer: *John Edeen*
Printer and binder: *R. R. Donnelley & Son*s

Library of Congress Card Catalog No. 92–62019

CONTENTS

PREFACE
TO THE INSTRUCTOR

Today we are used to hearing stories about the unethical use of information technology (IT): violations of data confidentiality, software piracy, and computer viruses are primary examples. Every day IT offers us new opportunities to compete more effectively. At the same time, the misuse of technology clearly has increased the threat to individuals and organizations from financial loss, tarnished reputations, and legal action.

Ethical Decision Making and Information Technology: An Introduction with Cases is designed to challenge this threat. It is designed for use as a supplement for any information systems course that shares our commitment to teach business students how to recognize, evaluate, and react responsibly to ethical dilemmas, and how to behave ethically themselves.

BUILDING A CONCEPTUAL FOUNDATION

This text assumes no prerequisites. Chapter 1 defines ethics, and introduces an ethical decision-making process. Chapter 2 relates ethics to IT. Chapter 3 applies a four-step analysis process to a real-world ethical dilemma involving IT, illustrating how to reach defensible ethical decisions. These introductory chapters equip students to evaluate the 18 real-world cases in Part II intelligently and systematically.

THE CASES

The 18 cases in this book have been class-tested and developed over four semesters by 14 information systems instructors, most of them new to teaching ethics. They are based on actual situations; only the names of the people and organizations have been changed. Dialogue has been included to enhance the realism of the case. The cases provide a blend of essential and nonessential facts that challenges students to separate "the wheat from the chaff," one of the fundamental skills developed by **Ethical Decision Making and Information Technology.**

To offer instructors flexibility, the cases cover a variety of topics. The table below delineates the 18 cases according to major ethical issues and appropriate course use. The accompanying *Instructor's Manual* includes guidelines for customizing the cases to specific course objectives.

Case Matrix

This table illustrates the flexibility of the 18 cases in this book. Each case is characterized by the key issues raised and possible course use.

CASE	TITLE	KEY ISSUES	COURSE(S)
1	Levity or Libel?	Misuse of company resources Accountability for actions	Data Communications Office Automation MIS Intro to IS
2	Credit Woes	Accuracy Credit bureaus	Database MIS Intro to IS
3	Something for Everyone?	Privacy Data recombination	Data Structures Database MIS Intro to IS
4	Abort, Retry, Ignore	Unauthorized access Whistle blowing Data access	Operating Systems Security and Privacy MIS Intro to IS

CASE	TITLE	KEY ISSUES	COURSE(S)
5	Messages from All Over	Inappropriate use of resources E-Mail	Data Communications Policy Network Management MIS Intro to IS
6	A Job on the Side	Duty Respect Consulting responsibilities	Systems Analysis System Design MIS Intro to IS
7	The New Job	Inappropriate use of resources Offensive startup screen Sexual harassment	Small Business Systems MIS Intro to IS
8	The Buyout	Privacy Data access	Security and Privacy Policy MIS Intro to IS
9	Charades	Password theft Duty Misuse of authority and power Lack of respect	Security and Privacy Operating Systems MIS Intro to IS
10	Laccaria and Eagle	Gray market International trade Protectionist measures	Policy Small Business Systems MIS Intro to IS
11	Taking Bad with Good	Premature software release Unprofessional behavior Virus released in retribution	System Design Policy Data Communications MIS Intro to IS
12	The Engineer and the Teacher	Power in society Poor school vs. rich engineering firm Software piracy	Intro to Computers Security and Privacy MIS Intro to IS

CASE	TITLE	KEY ISSUES	COURSE(S)
13	Test Data	Ethics of development Breaking trust Keeping quiet	Systems Analysis System Design MIS Intro to IS
14	The Brain Pick	Knowledge engineering	Artificial Intelligence Expert Systems MIS Intro to IS
15	Trouble in Sardonia	Copyrights International policy	Policy Security and Privacy MIS Intro to IS
16	Downtime	Ethical impact study Overdependence on computers Arrogance of IS professionals	System Design MIS Intro to IS
17	Code Blue	Privacy Technical limitations	Systems Analysis System Design Policy MIS Intro to IS
18	Virtual Success	The "dark side" Expert systems Artificial intelligence Virtual reality	Virtual Reality Artificial Intelligence MIS Intro to IS

DISTINGUISHING FEATURES

- **Assumes No Prerequisites:** Part I equips students with a conceptual foundation designed to help them recognize, evaluate, and react responsibly to the ethical dilemmas in each case study.

- **Flexible:** Supplements any information systems text. While providing sufficient detail for robust analysis, each two-page case can be discussed within a single class period. Instructors can mix and match the cases most appropriate to their specific course objectives.

- **Real World:** The 18 cases are based on actual events. They raise a variety of ethical dilemmas, and can be used in courses as illustrated in the Case Matrix.

- **Comprehensive Instructor's Manual:** Written with instructors new to teaching ethics in mind, this manual includes: Case Objectives, Key Ethical Issues, Discussion Ideas, Guidelines for Assigning and Evaluating Cases, and Strategies for Managing Classroom Discussion.

A FINAL COMMENT

By emphasizing the need for information systems professionals and users to behave ethically, we do not wish to imply that these individuals are less ethical than those in any other profession. Although the cases included in this book depict individuals often committing inappropriate acts, in reality, such actions are performed by a small percentage of users of IT. And, as we remind students, *most of the unethical activity that does occur has resulted because individuals did not realize an act was unethical or did not know how to make ethical decisions.*

ACKNOWLEDGMENTS

A special thanks to the graduate students in the Bentley College MSCIS program who, through their personal and professional experiences, discovered the ethical situations that are the basis of most of the cases in this book. We congratulate them for their sensitivity to ethical situations and their commitment to ethical computer use. We especially thank the following graduates for their willingness to share their episodes:

Ronald Anderson, CMA; Scott Bickford; Donna Boggs; Miriam Boucher; Michael Carmen, MSCIS; Laura Carpenter, RN; David Carr; Paul Cormier; Richard Creeden; Gilbert DeCosta; Nicholas Di Ciaccio; Michael Drake; Karen Estle-Verma; Brian Fahey; Karen Finocchio; Judith Gagne; Leonard Hand, Jr.; Bob Hoban; John Hubley; Eric Lanchenal; Janet Lewis; Wendy McAvoy; Mary McDonagh; Lauren Merz; Joseph O'Connor; Raymond Pace; Joel Plotnick; Francis Quinn; Gerardo Santos,

MS; Ronald Saulnier; Susan Schwab; M. Alison Stoddart; John Tarvin; Paul Thornton; Maxine Poche Troy; and Thai Truong, MSCIS.

Additional thanks are due to the following for their advice and counsel:

J. J. Bloombecker, National Center for Computer Crime Data
Roy M. Dejoie, Texas A&M University
B. Loerinc Helft, Baruch College
Thomas Hilton, Utah State University
Karen-Ann Kievit, Loyola Marymount University
Marianne LaFrance, Boston College
Jennifer Wagner, Roosevelt University
Mary B. Williams, University of Delaware

To the following for their perseverance in wading through rough drafts of this book:

Dave Callaghan
Bill McKinnon
Sandy Sherizen
Jeff Smith
Bill VanderClock

To the Bentley CIS Faculty who have class-tested the cases and made significant contributions to the *Instructor's Manual:*

Dennis Anderson   Paul Plourde
Don Chand   Mary Ann Robbert
Irv Englander   Doug Robertson
John Gorgone   Satya Saraswat
Jane Huerta   Les Waguespack
Jim Linderman   Coralee Whitcomb
Ido Millet   Hank Zbyszynski

Also, kudos to some special people in the Bentley Center for Business Ethics for their guidance, education, and encouragement:

Mike Hoffman, Director
Bob Frederick
Frank Reeves

Finally, we would like to give special thanks to Toni Murray, our copy-editor, who added style and grace to our prose.

Ernest Kallman
Bentley College

John Grillo
Bentley College

APPROACHES TO ETHICAL DECISION MAKING

The objectives of the chapters in Part I are to:

- Raise sensitivity to ethical circumstances involving information technology—circumstances that have the potential to harm individuals, organizations, or society.

- Provide a process for analyzing ethical situations and for making decisions in response to them.

- Instill in each reader a readiness and a willingness to accept responsibility for the ethicality of his or her actions.

ETHICS IS NOT A FOUR-LETTER WORD

An Explanation of Ethics and Ethical Decision Making

WHY WE SHOULD CARE ABOUT ETHICS

Ethics is the practice of making a principled choice between right and wrong. Ethical dilemmas occur in business as well as in our personal lives. We hear about them on TV, on the job, and in school, and we read about them in the popular press. More and more, the ethical situations seem to involve computers and other forms of information technology, a field that includes computers, telecommunications, and video.

When the situations involve us personally, we can often influence their resolution. But to exercise positive influence, we must understand both the nature of the problem and how to analyze it. The easy part is understanding the problem. Even in situations involving computers, this does not necessarily mean knowing a great deal about technology. The more difficult task is attacking the problem logically and making decisions based on defensible ethical principles.

For a responsible person, ethical principles are an essential part of solving the problem. Ethical principles are ideas of behavior that are commonly acceptable to society. Using ethical principles as a basis for decision making prevents us from relying only on intuition or personal preference.

Why should we care about ethics? The number of ethical choices that face us every day makes it imperative that we care. Obviously, some unethical actions—even if made unwittingly—can put us on the wrong side of the law. Other unethical actions, though not illegal, can have drastic consequences for our careers and reputations. Therefore, each of us must care about ethics as a matter of self-interest. Knowing the principles of ethical decision making is a cultural survival skill. In addition, each person who benefits from living in society has an obligation to uphold the principles on which it is based. Therefore, ethical decision making is vital to creating a world in which we want to live.

This chapter will explain what ethics has to do with information technology, how ethics relates to human action, how to choose between right and wrong, how to choose between two "rights," where laws come in, and how to use a number of guidelines and ethical principles to make ethical decisions.

COMPUTER ETHICS
AND REGULAR ETHICS

Is "computer ethics," or ethics regarding information technology, really different from "regular" ethics? Is there an ethical difference between browsing through someone else's computer file and browsing through their desk drawer? Most experts agree that there is actually no special category of computer ethics; rather, there are ethical situations in which computers are involved. The capabilities of the computer often lend a special character to problems of computer ethics, however. For instance, the computer often allows people to perform unethical actions faster or to perform actions that were too difficult or impossible using manual methods. The fact that computers are now so common makes organizations and individuals increasingly vulnerable to their unethical use.

The fact is that some people do browse through computer files when they are not authorized to do so. And some people who use computers and who develop systems for computers perform numerous other unethical and illegal activities. Activities such as violation of copyright and invasion of privacy threaten to harm both individuals and organizations. The problem will get worse as the number of computers increases, as more people use them, and as the computers assume more critical roles in the organizations that employ them.

Another characteristic common to computer ethics is the difficulty of identifying ethical issues. Many of those who perform unethical practices with computers do not see the ethical implications. Their first reaction when caught is "I didn't know I did anything wrong. I only looked at the file. I didn't take it." If they copy a file, they say, "I didn't do anything wrong. The file is still there for the owner. I just made a copy." Hackers often say, "I was just testing to see how secure the system was. I was going to report the weakness to management. I was performing a valuable service." One of the major objectives of this book is to increase your sensitivity to ethical issues involving computers so that you will recognize the issues when you see them. (This is, in fact, the purpose of Chapter 2.)

As later sections of this chapter will discuss, a third characteristic of computer ethics is the wide array of ethical dilemmas the computer presents. The computer user and developer are routinely faced with a range of ethical options from illegal to not nice.

Computer ethics should have a strong link to policy or strategy. Once an ethical problem is identified, a policy or strategy should be developed to prevent the problem from recurring.

COMPETING FACTORS IN DECISION MAKING

At the biological level, human beings are directed by the drives for food, shelter, and love. On another level, we are guided by laws, which we accept as the rules established by some group, such as Congress, a church, or culture. At a higher and more abstract level, our behavior is modified by our understanding of what is good, right, proper, moral, or *ethical*.

Human action is rarely simple or straightforward. At any one time, influences from several levels affect our behavior. These influences often lead to competing outcomes, so an individual must weigh risks and consequences before making an independent value judgment about how to act.

Decisions involving information technology incorporate as many levels as other decisions. In addition to involving personal needs and desires and public values, decisions about computer technology typically involve many shades of gray—possibilities that, by social standards, are not exclusively right or wrong.

THE CONSEQUENCES OF POOR VALUE JUDGMENTS

Value judgments are really personal or business decisions in which ethics has a bearing on the choice to be made. The risk in situations involving ethics is the risk of poor judgment. A poor judgment, or low-quality decision, can have a wide range of results: It can hurt a person's feelings, lower employee morale, cause a business to lose customers, decrease profits, or cause a firm to be sued or go bankrupt. In addition, poor judgment can have negative effects for society—by destroying confidence in public officials, for example.

All people make ethical decisions. Organizations would probably come to a standstill without them. But what is ethics? It's not religion. It's not preaching or making people believe as you do. Ethics is the practice of making principled choices.

THE TYPES OF ETHICAL CHOICES

One type of ethical choice involves choosing right from wrong. Another type involves choosing right from right.

Choosing Right from Wrong

Most of us know that stealing, lying, and cheating are wrong. These three actions are the taboos of a commonsense morality. For instance, if we take the hotel towels, we know we are stealing and that the act is wrong. If we swear to the judge that we were going 55 miles per hour when we were actually going 75, we know we are lying and that the act is wrong. You can probably describe half a dozen such situations in as many minutes.

Choosing Right from Right

But ethical choices get harder when the situation is not as clear, is not black or white, but contains some gray. Lying may be wrong. But when we visit a sick friend, is it wrong to exaggerate how well he or she looks? We may be lying about the person's condition, but we are probably doing it to achieve what we perceive to be a higher good: the quick recovery or general welfare of the patient. Is it wrong for me to steal food if I am starving? Is it wrong if my child is starving? Is it wrong to keep any coins you find in a pay telephone? Does the money belong to the previous caller? To the phone company? To you? Does the amount make a difference? (Keep a small amount, return a large amount?) How would you give the coins back? Do you call the operator and offer to feed the coins back into the machine? What if the operator will not take them? Are you off the hook, so to speak? Should you give all the money to charity?

These examples of visiting a sick friend or handling a telephone bonanza, however trivial, are typical of the structure of many ethical situations. They illustrate the complexity of *ethical choice*—the necessity to choose a course of action from two or more alternatives, each having some desirable result. In other words, in an ethical choice, an individual must often choose between two or more "goods" or the lesser of two "evils," or between two or more paths to achieve some desirable objective. These choices are often impacted by any number of contingencies with varying degrees of relevance.

To explore the problem of choosing among alternatives that are neither wholly right nor wholly wrong, consider the following ethical dilemmas:

- How much security do we impose on computer files? To make sign-on procedures easier and encourage system use, do we leave certain data files vulnerable to browsing (which may invade the privacy of some employees or clients and cause them harm)? Or do we protect the data better and lose those users (or customers) who will not be bothered to wade through the tighter controls? In other words, is the objective user friendliness or data protection? How much user friendliness are we willing to sacrifice for data protection, or how much risk to data confidentiality are we willing to take to foster user friendliness? This is a choice between two goods.

- New software is promised, and sorely needed, by a specific date. The project is late. Do we install software that is not fully tested? If so, do we inform the client or user? Do we install software with less functionality than promised? If so, do we inform the client or user? Do we "bust the budget" and work overtime to meet the deadline? Do we ask for an extension? In this case, there is a worthwhile objective, meeting the deadline, with more than one path to its achievement.

These kinds of ethical situations—which include competing interests, each with some merit—are the most difficult to handle. Even after the ethical choice is made, we may have to make an additional effort to convince those on the other side that the choice was the best one for all concerned.

PRACTICAL APPROACHES TO ETHICAL DECISION MAKING

All of us address ethical decisions with some sense of right and wrong acquired in our upbringing. But many, especially young people, have had few opportunities to test their convictions. They may never have had to make the hard choice between taking the consequences of their convictions and avoiding the issue. They may never have had to choose between giving up a good job but acting ethically, and agreeing to perform some unethical act to keep that job. They may never have had to wrestle with what to do when they found out that someone else was acting unethically. For this reason, it is important to learn how to evaluate ethical situations and make defensible decisions.

Notice the phrase used is "defensible decisions," not "right decisions." Two honest individuals can examine the same ethical situation and arrive at different courses of action. But a high-quality ethical decision is based on reason and can be defended according to ethical concepts. By applying one or more ethical concepts to a situation, a person can rationally examine alternative options and choose the best one.

Making ethical decisions is by no means a science. People do it differently. In one sense, all ethical questions could be answered with that most ubiquitous of responses: It all depends. But in ethical decision making, the individual must decide what the answer does depend on: what the facts are, what harm might be done by each alternative, and which course results in the least harm. There are some ways to help an individual do this. The next sections will discuss how laws, guidelines, and ethical principles contribute to making ethical choices.

Using Law to Make Ethical Decisions

When a law tells us to do or not to do something, it implies that a recognized authority has decided that the action the law prescribes is of benefit to society in some way. You may well ask, "What was the basis for any decision regarding this issue before this law was written?" It often happens that an ethical principle was used prior to a law's construction. As you recall, ethical principles are ideas of behavior that are commonly acceptable to society.

For example, the generally accepted ethical principle that we should help others in need leads to specific Good Samaritan laws that protect the rights of individuals who help an injured person. In the computer field the principle of recognizing an individual's right to ownership of an original work has led to copyright laws that protect software.

The fact that law is grounded in ethical principle makes law a good starting point for ethical decision making. In other words, when we are confronted with an ethical decision, we should first look to see what the law says. In some instances, the law will clearly apply and lead directly to the appropriate ethical choice. However, in many situations, the law will not lead to a straightforward solution. There are bad laws, and there are times when individuals may rightfully choose to disobey the law. The relationship between ethics and law leads to four possible states that depend on whether a specific act is ethical or not ethical (unethical), and legal or not legal (illegal). The table that follows presents these states visually.

Legality versus Ethicality

	LEGAL	NOT LEGAL
Ethical	I	II
Not ethical	III	IV

Source: Wagner, Jennifer L. Using a taxonomy of ethical situations in MIS, *1991 Journal/Proceedings Information Systems and Quantitative Management*, Midwest Business Administration Association, 1991, 112–118.

I = An act that is ethical and legal
II = An act that is ethical but not legal
III = An act that is not ethical but is legal
IV = An act that is not ethical and not legal

The outline that follows presents examples of each category of action presented in the preceding table. Note that the categorization of the situations offers much room for disagreement.

I.   Ethical and legal
   ▪ Firing an individual who does not perform according to expectations or who fails to follow certain contractual obligations
   ▪ Increasing the price of goods when the demand for those goods increases
   ▪ Buying Lotus 1-2-3 and using it to do accounting for clients

II. Ethical but not legal
   ▪ Copying copyrighted software to use only as a backup, even when the copyright agreement specifically prohibits copying for that purpose

- Using civil disobedience to attract attention to a "just" cause
III.   Not ethical but legal
   - Revealing data that was expected to remain confidential—for example, gossiping, by data entry operators, about the salary data they are processing
   - Using a pirated version of Lotus 1-2-3 in a foreign country that has no software copyright laws
   - Distributing mailing lists or other legally obtained personal information, without the knowledge of the people on the lists

IV.   Not ethical and not legal
   - Pirating copyrighted software
   - Planting viruses in someone else's computer system

As stated, people often have differing views of these legal-versus-ethical situations. Maybe you would object to firing an individual in a certain case while someone else would feel that firing was the "right" thing to do. Perhaps your understanding of a "just" cause conflicts with another person's; therefore, each of you would act differently in the same situation. Often, arguments on both sides of ethical issues are defensible.

When the law does not provide an answer, as when the dilemma falls in categories II or III, it is sometimes useful to consider an ethical dilemma by using formal or informal guidelines. The next sections present such guidelines.

Using Formal Guidelines to Make Ethical Decisions

A guideline is an outline for conduct. Violating a guideline does not necessarily have the legal implications of breaking a law. A formal guideline is an explicit statement. Examples include a statement of corporate policy, an association's code of ethics, or any list of decision-making criteria whose purpose is to foster acceptable behavior.

Figure 1–1 presents the Code of Ethics and Professional Conduct of the Association for Computing Machinery (ACM). The ACM is a professional society of more that 85,000 members whose purpose is to foster understanding about information technology and standards for its use.

The list of questions that follows is also a formal guideline—one you may find helpful in solving the ethical problems you face as an information professional. The responses to various questions may give contradictory advice. But, by working through the questions, you can gain a clear picture of the dilemma and—perhaps—the beginnings of an ethical solution.

FIGURE 1–1   The ACM Code of Ethics and Professional Conduct*

PREAMBLE

Commitment to professional conduct is expected of every member (voting members, associate members, and student members) of the Association for Computing Machinery (ACM). This code identifies several issues professionals are likely to face, and provides guidelines for dealing with them. Section 1 presents fundamental ethical considerations, while Section 2 addresses additional considerations of professional conduct. Statements in Section 3 pertain more specifically to individuals who have a leadership role, whether in the workplace or in a professional organization such as ACM. Guidelines for encouraging compliance with this Code are given in Section 4.

1. **General Moral Imperatives**

    As an ACM member, I will . . .

    1.1 Contribute to society and human well-being,

    1.2 Avoid harm to others,

    1.3 Be honest and trustworthy,

    1.4 Be fair and take action not to discriminate,

    1.5 Honor property rights including copyrights and patents,

    1.6 Give proper credit for intellectual property,

    1.7 Access computing and communication resources only when authorized to do so,

    1.8 Respect the privacy of others,

    1.9 Honor confidentiality.

2. **More Specific Professional Responsibilities**

    As an ACM computing professional, I will . . .

    2.1 Strive to achieve the highest quality in both the process and products of professional work,

    2.2 Acquire and maintain professional competence,

    2.3 Know and respect existing laws pertaining to professional work,

    2.4 Accept and provide appropriate professional review,

    2.5 Give comprehensive and thorough evaluations of computer systems and their impacts, with special emphasis on possible risks,

    2.6 Honor contracts, agreements, and assigned responsibilities,

    2.7 Improve public understanding of computing and its consequences.

3. **Organizational Leadership Imperatives**

    As an ACM member and an organizational leader, I will . . .

    3.1 Articulate social responsibilities of members of an organizational unit and encourage full acceptance of those responsibilities,

    3.2 Manage personnel and resources to design and build information systems that enhance the quality of working life,

    3.3 Acknowledge and support proper and authorized uses of an organization's computing and communication resources,

3.4 Ensure that users and those who will be affected by a system have their needs clearly articulated during the assessment and design of requirements, and that later the system must be validated to meet requirements,

3.5 Articulate and support policies that protect the dignity of users and others affected by a computing system,

3.6 Create opportunities for members of the organization to learn the principles and limitations of computer systems.

4. Compliance with the Code

As an ACM member, I will . . .

4.1 Uphold and promote the principles of this Code,

4.2 Agree to take appropriate action leading to a remedy if the Code is violated,

4.3 Treat violations of this code as inconsistent with membership in the ACM.

*Draft revision, February 12, 1992, *Communications of the ACM*, May 1992, 94–95.

1. Is the act consistent with corporate policy? Either explicitly or implicitly, corporations often tell their employees how to act. The policy may be a rule stating that no gifts are to be accepted from vendors, or it may just be a motto, such as "The customer is always right." Both these policies are guides to individual action.

2. Does the act violate corporate or professional codes of conduct or ethics? Often companies and professional organizations adopt such codes. Some are quite specific and can be helpful in directing the activities of the members. Even if you do not belong to a professional society or your organization does not have a computer ethics code, it may be worthwhile to adopt a code as your personal guide.

3. Does the act violate the Golden Rule? That is, are you treating others the way you would wish them to treat you?

4. Does the act serve the majority rather than a minority? Does it serve yourself only? Generally, an outcome that benefits the majority, or serves the common good, is more desirable than one that benefits a few or even one.

Using Informal Guidelines to Make Ethical Decisions

Informal guidelines allow us to quickly evaluate a situation in an attempt to resolve an ethical dilemma. By using informal guidelines, a decision maker can often arrive at a general direction for ethical action.

This section presents a number of tests that you can use to approach ethical problems.

The Mom Test

Would you tell your mother what you did? This test simply discovers whether you would be proud or ashamed of an action. The Mom Test uses a highly personal reaction as the first indicator of a problem. For example, suppose you write a "word shock" program that makes up phrases and sentences from a pool of words the dictionary defines as vulgar. Would you brag to your mom about it, or would you try to keep her from finding out?

The TV Test

How would you feel if you saw your situation described on TV or in the *New York Times*? Would the story make you look good or bad? How would the millions of viewers or readers react? In this test, pretend your ethical dilemma is being publicized far and wide. For example, let's say you and your very best friend are competing computer graphics consultants but, to save money, you decide to share copies of all software. How would an article describing your decision reflect on your business and you?

The Smell Test

Does the situation "smell"? Do you just feel in your bones that there's a problem, but you can't pin it down? If so, there is a problem, because the situation has failed the Smell Test. For example, suppose you develop a program that takes text and paraphrases it in any style you choose. On the surface this program seems relatively innocent, but something just doesn't feel right. When you think about it at length, you discover potential problems: What if someone takes Mark Twain's works and uses your program to rewrite them in the style of Hawthorne? Could the customer produce a "long-lost Hawthorne manuscript"? What else might happen?

The Other Person's Shoes Test

What if the roles were reversed? Would you be happy if the act were done to you, if you were in the other person's shoes? This test discovers actions that violate the ethical concept of the public interest. If you wouldn't want the roles reversed, then there is probably something wrong. For example, suppose your company develops a database management system that your client wants desperately—indeed, the client is even willing to pay a bonus for early release. You know there are bugs in the program as it is now, but you decide to sell it early anyway and use the bonus to debug the product more quickly. Then you can send your client a new version. Would you like to be the client? If not, the situation fails the Other Person's Shoes Test.

The Market Test

Would you use your behavior as a marketing tool? In other words, does your action have enough merit to give you a marketing edge? Suppose the database management system you were developing in the previous section is completed early, and it contains only a few "work-around" bugs that you can describe to your client. Would you consider its early sale, in that condition, to be a marketing advantage? If not, early sale would fail the Market Test.

So far, this chapter has presented practical approaches to ethical decisions—formal and informal guidelines you can apply to solve problems. Sometimes, however, the practical approach is not broad enough to solve a problem. Those who are best equipped to solve ethical dilemmas have a knowledge of the academic philosophies of ethics as well as the practical approaches. The sections that follow will introduce you to several of these philosophies: the principle of harm minimization, the study of rights and duties, the principles of consequentialism, and Kant's idea of the categorical imperative.

THE PRINCIPLE OF HARM MINIMIZATION

A common standard for deciding right from wrong, the principle of harm minimization prescribes choosing the course of action that minimizes the amount of harm. If you, as an individual, make this principle part of your everyday toolkit, you may discover that it affords you an unexpected advantage. Bearing the principle of harm minimization in mind is likely to help you spot ethical problems as well as solve them.

Sometimes it is helpful to examine ethical dilemmas from the stakeholder's perspective. A *stakeholder* is any person or organization with a stake in the decision. *Harm* refers to any act, physical or psychological, that denies a stakeholder his or her reasonable rights. Using the harm-minimization principle, an ethical activity is one that minimizes harm to stakeholders. (You must remember, however, that different stakeholders may have different—and competing—concerns and interests.) An unethical activity is one that results in unnecessary harm or an activity that has the potential for harm.

HOW RIGHTS AND DUTIES RELATE TO ETHICS*

The study of rights and duties is called deontology. The term comes from the Greek word *deon*, which means duty. Having an understanding of rights and duties is helpful in analyzing ethical situations and making an ethical choice. The notion of responsibility is a part of this discussion.

Considering Rights

Rights are inherent universal privileges—privileges that we consider our due by reason of law, tradition, or nature. The Constitution's Bill of Rights, for example, safeguards important political rights. The field of information technology frequently involves questions about three specific rights:

- *The right to know:* To what extent do we have a right to know, and have access to, the information that relates to us in a database? What rights do other people have to know and access the information that relates to them if it exists in our database?

- *The right to privacy:* To what extent do we have a right to control the dissemination of information that pertains to us? For example, should our personal medical information be accessible only to the people we authorize to use it? What privacy rights do others have in regard to the data we hold about them?

- *The right to property:* To what extent do we have a right to protect our computer resources from misuse and abuse? For example, what measures can we take to prevent viruses from being planted or our software from being copied?

Considering Duties

When one does something because it is a duty, he or she feels compelled by a moral obligation—the action cannot be avoided. All human beings, according to the world's moralists, have certain duties in common. These duties are the basis for our definition of rights. If a person has rights, he or she also has

---

*This discussion and the discussion of consequentialism are based on discussions at The Ethics Gadfly Workshop. The workshop was held at the Center for Business Ethics, Bentley College, Waltham, Massachusetts, during the summer of 1991. Dr. W. Michael Hoffman and Dr. M. Francis Reeves conducted the workshop under a grant from the General Electric Corporation.

corresponding duties—duties that are expected of an individual in society. The basic duty is harm minimization, which includes the duty not to cause unnecessary harm. The principle of harm minimization was explained earlier in this chapter.

A concept closely related to duty is responsibility, which is a duty that is usually well defined and specific to a profession. Information professionals have the duties we all have as individuals, and they have professional responsibilities, which are described in various codes of ethics.

Personal Duties

The moral obligations in the list that follows are common to almost all cultures. They form the basis for most of the value-laden judgments that a human being makes.

Each person has the personal duty:

- *To foster trust:* Trust occurs when others have confidence that our work is competent, timely, and will not cause harm.

- *To act with integrity:* Acting with integrity allows others to depend on our honesty.

- *To be truthful:* Others should be able to expect us to be truthful and to act with fidelity.

- *To do justice:* Justice is served when our dealings with others are fair. Justice demands that those who perform services are rightfully paid and that wrongful acts are deservedly punished.

- *To practice beneficence and nonmaleficence:* Acts of beneficence help others improve their lot. Nonmaleficence prohibits causing harm to others.

- *To act with appropriate gratitude and make appropriate reparation:* Gratitude is being thankful for the kind acts of others; reparation is the act of providing fair recompense for wrongful acts done to them.

- *To work toward self-improvement:* When we improve our moral and mental faculties, such as by not committing a wrong a second time, we are acting according to the duty of self-improvement.

Professional Responsibilities

When a person accepts employment in any position, he or she accepts moral responsibilities that define appropriate behavior in that job. These responsibilities are often referred to as professional ethics. Two factors apply to all professionals and influence their actions: professional relationships and professional efficacy. Most professions have ethical codes or standards that explain appropriate professional relationships and efficacious behavior in various situations, and the computer profession is no different. Information professionals have the additional responsibilities of maintaining confidentiality and impartiality.

Professional Relationships   As professionals, we have relationships with employers, clients, co-workers, and others. These relationships are different from our relationships with parents, spouse, and friends. For one thing, professional relationships may be specifically defined, even in a written contract. They are carried out within a framework of laws, customs, and policies. For example, an employee has a responsibility to perform a full day's work. The corresponding duty on the part of the employer is to reward that work equitably.

Professional Efficacy   As professionals, we have some skill or knowledge through which we produce some product or service. Because we have this power, we have also the obligation to use it in a way that reduces harm or increases the public good. For example, a computer consultant proposes a new system with a one-year development period. The client claims to need the system in six months. The professional knows that a system delivered that soon will not do the job and may, in fact, cause serious harm to the client and those the client serves. Professional efficacy demands that the consultant explain the reality to the client and, if necessary, refuse the assignment.

Confidentiality and Impartiality   Two examples of responsibilities typically expected from information systems professionals are confidentiality and impartiality.

Confidentiality demands that a professional protect information from unauthorized access and use. Consider this situation: Thomas is a financial analyst who uses a computer terminal daily to access information about stocks and bonds. One day he discovers that his terminal can also access the medical database that contains information about his fellow employees. He has no need for this information in the daily performance of his job. His *duty* is to notify his superior that he has access to this database, because it is providing an avenue for violating the confidentiality that his fellow employees have a *right* to expect.

Impartiality demands that a professional be fair and impartial, treating all parties equally so that professional services can be provided without bias. For instance, impartiality demands that a software firm make new releases available to all customers, on the same basis.

CONSEQUENTIALISM

When we focus on the goals, ends, results, or consequences of an action, we are using the principle of consequentialism. Another word for consequentialism is *teleology*, which comes from the Greek word *telos*, or goal. We judge the rightness or wrongness of an action by the outcomes. Two major types of consequentialism are egoism and utilitarianism. Egoism focuses on self-interest; utilitarianism focuses on the public interest.

Deciding Ethical Questions Through Egoism

Egoism refers to the concept of long-term rationality, which is also called enlightened self-interest or prudence. If an action doesn't help you in the long term, it is foolish, or imprudent. We use this ethical principle as justification when we do something that furthers our own welfare. It is sometimes helpful to think of this as the "good for me" principle or the "ethics of arrogance," because we may subordinate higher-quality ethical outcomes to those that serve our own advantage. On the other hand, self-interest, in the form of a company seeking to increase its profits, is a valid justification for many business actions. This is an illustration of the kind of ambiguity that can result in ethical analysis—that is, egoism may be justified in certain circumstances and not in others. A decision maker who relies on a single principle without consideration of other principles may be led to inappropriate conclusions. Egoism needs to be *guided* and *limited* by other ethical principles.

If an individual feels threatened, either by having his or her actions detected or by the threat of punishment for those actions, egoism has probably been misapplied. The individual's actions may have passed the "good for me" test but are ethically insupportable because of possible harm to others.

For example, suppose you discover, in an obscure journal, a highly efficient algorithm for sorting records. You decide to incorporate it into your production software, and you take credit for it as your own idea. As a result, you feel threatened by the possible detection of your act and you fear punishment. In this case, you based your actions on self-interest only; the principle of egoism was not supported by any other principle. You did not consider the possible harm that your decision could cause to others. As you will see in the discussion of utilitarianism, you should consider all stakeholders in your analysis.

To return to the example of the premature release of database management software: Suppose many customers have already paid deposits, and some have paid the full price; they are desperate for this program. However, it hasn't been tested thoroughly, and now Alice, the product manager, has to decide whether the program should be released. She decides that her reputation is at stake, so she releases the program to the customers. Did she consider all stakeholders? Was she acting solely on the basis of her interests (the ethics of arrogance)? What are the consequences of her actions? What if all software developers always released their products on the advertised release date?

Deciding Ethical Questions Through Utilitarianism

When our actions benefit others as well as ourselves, we are operating in the public interest. We measure the usefulness, or utility, of our actions not only for ourselves, but for all stakeholders. This approach embodies the principle of utilitarianism, which helps a person judge, through a form of cost-benefit analysis, whether an action is ethical. An action is right if it maximizes benefits over costs for all involved, everyone counting equally.

For example, consider Alice, the manager of the software company already mentioned. Suppose she notifies all potential customers that the software will be delayed during an intensive period of beta testing. She has measured the importance of the reputation of her company against some possible lost sales and decided that the greater benefit lies in protecting the company's name. Also, by informing the customers of the delay, she is serving the public interest.

Now consider a company that provides sufficient security to protect the sensitive data files of its clients. The company is acting in accord with utilitarianism, even though it increases costs and lowers profits to the firm's stockholders.

KANT'S CATEGORICAL IMPERATIVE

Immanuel Kant suggested two principles for examining whether a person has the right to act a certain way in a given situation: consistency and respect. The principles of consistency and respect are aspects of what Kant called the categorical imperative.

Applying the Principle of Consistency

Would it make sense to force everyone to take the action being studied? If not, do not take it. For example, if everyone lied, how would we ever know the truth? Or, if everyone copied software rather than buying it, how could we expect anyone to offer software for sale?

Applying the Principle of Respect

This principle suggests that we treat people with dignity—that people are ends in themselves, not means. If we use people as slaves, we deny their humanness and do not show them respect. Thus, slavery violates the categorical imperative. In the computer field, performing electronic surveillance on employees without their knowledge might be considered an act of disrespect and a violation of the categorical imperative.

SUMMARY

Everyone has the obligation to understand ethics. Making ethical choices is part of everyday life, especially for those who use and create information technology. Ethical situations involving computers take many forms. Often, those in the situations do not realize ethics is involved.

In making ethical choices, following a logical approach usually leads to higher-quality decisions than one that relies on intuition or personal preference alone. A logical approach—whether it employs a formal or informal guideline or an academic theory—tries in some way to answer the following questions:

- Does the action serve the public interest or, at least, not cause unnecessary social harm?

- Are any basic human rights violated?

- Are any commonly accepted duties abridged?

The key to solving an ethical dilemma is to use as many logical approaches as possible to analyze the problem. Figure 1–2 summarizes the approaches presented in this chapter. Completing the four steps the figure cites may lead you to realize that there are several conflicting resolutions; the challenge is to balance the conflicts to produce the highest-quality decision possible.

FIGURE 1–2   A Guide to Ethical Decision Making

To approach an ethical choice logically:
1. Examine the legal issues.
2. Consult guidelines.
3. Discover applicable ethical principles.
4. Make a defensible ethical choice based on your conclusions from the preceding steps.

1. Examine the legal issues. Actions can be:
   - Ethical and legal
   - Ethical but not legal
   - Not ethical but legal
   - Not ethical and not legal
2. Consult guidelines
   a. Formal guidelines
      Formal guidelines include corporate policies, codes of ethics, and other lists of decision-making criteria. Such guidelines usually call for asking the following questions:
      - Is the act consistent with corporate policy?
      - Does the act violate corporate or professional codes of conduct or ethics?
      - Does the act violate the Golden Rule?
      - Does it serve the majority rather than a minority?
   b. Informal guidelines
      Tests for rightness or wrongness
      - *Mom Test:* Would you tell her?
      - *TV Test:* Would you tell a nationwide audience?
      - *Smell Test:* Does the situation "smell"?
      - *Other Person's Shoes Test:* What if the roles were reversed?
      - *Market Test:* Could you advertise the act to gain a marketing edge?
3. Discover the applicable ethical principles
   a. The principle of harm minimization
      Choose the action that minimizes actual and potential harm.
   b. Principles involving rights and duties (deontology)
      (1) Rights include
          - The right to know
          - The right to privacy
          - The right to property
      (2) Duties
          Personal duties
          - Trust
          - Integrity

- Truthfulness
- Justice
- Beneficence and nonmaleficence
- Gratitude and reparation
- Self-improvement

Professional responsibilities
- For all professionals:
  Maintain appropriate professional relationships.
  Maintain professional efficacy.
- For information professionals in particular:
  Maintain confidentiality.
  Maintain impartiality.

   c. Principles involving consequentialism (teleology)
      (1) Egoism
      (2) Utilitarianism
   d. Kant's categorical imperative
      (1) The principle of consistency
      (2) The principle of respect

4. Make a defensible ethical choice
   Review the conclusions reached in the preceding steps and ask:
   - Does the action serve the public interest or, at least, not cause unnecessary social harm?
   - Are any basic human rights violated?
   - Are any commonly accepted duties abridged?

REFERENCES

ACM code of ethics and professional conduct, *Communications of the ACM*, May 1992, 94–99.

Andrews, Kenneth R. Ethics in practice, *Harvard Business Review*, September–October 1989, 99–104.

Bologna, Jack. A framework for the ethical analysis of information technologies, *Computers & Security*, October 1991, 303–307.

Carroll, Archie B. In search of the moral manager, *Business Horizons*, March–April 1987, 7–15.

Johnson, Deborah. *Computer Ethics*, Englewood Cliffs, NJ: Prentice-Hall, 1985.

Laczniak, G. Business ethics: A manager's primer, *Business*, January/March 1983, 23–29.

Murphy, Patrick E. Implementing business ethics, *Journal of Business Ethics*, vol. 7, 1988, 907–915.

Wagner, Jennifer L. Using a taxonomy of ethical situations in MIS, *1991 Journal/Proceedings Information Systems and Quantitative Management*, Midwest Business Administration Association, 1991, 112–118.

CHAPTER 2

ETHICS AND INFORMATION TECHNOLOGY
Computers Don't Have Ethics, People Do

NEW TECHNOLOGY, NEW PROBLEMS

Computers have changed forever the way we conduct business and live our lives. Each new year of the Information Age means more and faster processing by smaller and more powerful computers. In their special way, computers have compressed time and space. Today, computers perform processes and provide services that were impossible yesterday. We can make airline reservations instantly, get cash from a teller machine, and send electronic mail around the world. Computer capabilities are still expanding and are not expected to level off in the foreseeable future.

The amazing abilities of computers present new ethical challenges. Chapter 1 mentioned a few characteristics that typify "computer" ethics. Chapter 2 will expand this discussion by showing how the unique natures of computers and humans contribute to ethical dilemmas. The chapter will then list ethical issues that pertain to specific aspects of information technology. Some of these issues—such as computer crime—are obvious. Others—such as an

employer's obligation to provide an ergonomic computing environment—
are less so. The purpose of this chapter is to sensitize you to all the aspects of
information technology that involve ethics. If at some future time you think
to yourself, "There is an ethical dilemma here, and I need to analyze it before
I go on," then the chapter will have achieved its goal.

WHY IS ETHICAL COMPUTER USE A SPECIAL CHALLENGE?

Managing computers ethically—that is, acting ethically and assisting others
to do likewise—is no easy task for either an individual or an organization.
Donn Parker, Susan Swope, and Bruce Baker (all of SRI International), claim
that "the application of ethics in information science, technology, and business is more difficult than in other disciplines" (Parker et al., 1990). In ex-
plaining why, the three authors cite several unique aspects of computers and
computer use.

The Difficulties That Computers Pose

Parker, Swope, and Baker offer several reasons why ethical problems involving computers pose a special challenge.

- Using computers and data communications alters the relationships
  among people. Personal contact is reduced, and the speed of communication often does not give the participant time to reflect on the possibility or
  implications of unethical use.

- When information is in electronic form, it is far more "fragile" than when
  it is on paper. It is more easily changed and more vulnerable to unauthorized access. The questions of property rights, plagiarism, piracy, and privacy become active issues.

- Efforts to protect information integrity, confidentiality, and availability
  often conflict with the desire for the benefits of information sharing.

- The lack of widespread means of authorization and authentication ex-
  poses information technology to unethical practice.

The computer's unique nature is only part of the reason why computer
ethics is so hard to enforce. Human nature contributes to ethical dilemmas, as
the following section will show.

The Difficulties That People Pose

Two concepts have a major effect on how humans perceive computers and, therefore, how humans perceive ethical situations involving computers. These concepts are the order-of-magnitude effect and the effort effect.

The Order-of-Magnitude Effect

Scientists and graphic artists are familiar with the order-of-magnitude effect. It is based on the fact that, for each tenfold increase (that is, an increase of one order of magnitude) in speed, our perception of what is going on changes dramatically. Consider, for example, the special-effects photographer's "fast motion" view of clouds building up in the sky. The photographer takes the shot at 2 frames per second instead of 24. That's roughly a difference of one order of magnitude in speed, and our perception of the clouds' movements is entirely different. Computers operate at a speed that is several orders of magnitude faster than human activity. This speed, of course, is why we use computers to manage many of our important affairs.

Our daily dealings with computers tend to mask the order-of-magnitude effect somewhat. The tenfold increases in power have occurred over a number of years, and our contact with the technology has been continuous. Much as human aging goes unnoticed from day to day, the power increases have happened without our being aware of them. Eventually, however, we must recognize these extraordinary advances in computer power and adapt our ethical stance accordingly. Consider these potential ethical hot spots, all related to the order-of-magnitude effect:

- Ten years ago, a database containing the names, addresses, and buying habits of 120 million people (more than the population of England and France combined) would have been too expensive and too large to create. Access to any worthwhile information would have been too slow. Today, such a database can fit on several CDs; its data can be accessed with a personal computer, and its cost is so low that a major software manufacturer considered such a database a real opportunity. Is it really inconceivable, then, that in 10 years we could have a "world database" of personal information about everyone? Who would have access to this world database? Everyone, or just a few? What would it be used for? How would it be controlled?

- Ten years ago, timesharing mainframe computers were still fairly new. Today, an individual with a personal computer can access many nationwide networks—often for an access fee of less than $100. How can we get ready for the "telenet" of the twenty-first century, which will connect us all electronically? What will its effect on privacy be? And what ethical dilemmas will accompany it?

- Five years ago, personal computer owners were thankful to have a 10-megabyte disk drive for under $1,000. For this amount today, we can buy a drive with 30 times that capacity, and it will be faster and more reliable than previous models when they were new. Is an affordable read/write optical disk with a gigabyte of storage in the near future? What are the implications of access to that much data? How can the data be massaged? Will new capabilities in video and voice processing create as yet un-anticipated security problems?

As a consequence of information technology's rapid growth, we are forced to adapt to its newest features on a continuing basis. There is pressure to keep up with the "cutting edge" so that our organizations are competitive. To use the deluge of new software and hardware takes extensive training. We can barely manage to learn the new technologies before they change and, as a result, we often pay scant attention to the consequences of their use.

The Effort Effect
The principle of unreasonable effort, or the effort effect, maintains that, if a task is not worth the effort, people will tend not to undertake it. Consider an example that relates to information technology. Using a manual system or even an early computer, a data file could be considered relatively secure because collating the data into some meaningful form was not worth the effort. In other words, even though access was not denied, privacy was ensured because wrongdoing required too much work. In addition, by the time the data was collated, it might well have lost its value.

If new technology changes the amount of work, however, people are likely to undertake new projects that use the technology. Newspaper reporters on one local paper provided an example of this. The reporters obtained computerized information about more than 30,000 state-subsidized mortgages. Through elementary computer processing they uncovered a scandal in the state mortgage agency. This could never have been detected by using only manual methods. The information had always been available, but it was "secure" because of the difficulty in using it.

With the order-of-magnitude effect and the effort effect in mind, now look more closely at specific unethical activity.

WHAT IS UNETHICAL COMPUTER USE?

Unethical computer use takes many forms, is performed by people inside and outside organizations, and occurs in regard to computers of all sizes and capabilities, both standalone and networked. Networked computers are much less secure because of their "outside" connection; therefore, they are much more vulnerable to unethical activity. But, in spite of the publicity that hackers have received, most unethical computer activity is performed by people inside a firm—quite often, by disgruntled employees. Furthermore, harm occurs and ethical problems arise not only in the use of the computer but in all the work of information systems professionals and those who work with them.

The remainder of this chapter will present, by category, specific ethical issues relating to information technology.

Social and Economic Issues

Job displacement caused by new information technology is an important ethical issue. Many who lose their jobs to "information machines" can be retrained, and the Information Age has required new professions, such as those of the computer programmer and systems analyst. But computers do cause displacement, and the ethical dilemma involves minimizing the hardship to those affected.

Another social aspect of computerization concerns the work-related demands placed on computer professionals. Computer work is pressure-filled; it always seems to be behind schedule. This results in long hours, often over weekends and holidays. Family problems and divorce rates are high in the profession. The ethical question: Is management being fair?

The third social issue involves power and access to it—in other words, civil rights. We have already shown that computers are part of our everyday existence. We need them to live the kind of lives we want to lead. But what of those who do not have access to computers? What about kids in an inner-city school system without computer courses? If the students are not computer literate, will they be able to compete on an equal footing with those who are? Do they have a right to equal computer access? Do they have less power than those who have access?

Issues of Individual Practice

Everyone who uses a computer has the responsibility to use it ethically. On an everyday level, this means each of us, as individuals, must use ethical practices. We must use passwords and change them frequently. We must not share passwords or choose ones that are so obvious that anyone could guess them. We must protect the computer resource by saving files periodically; backing up files regularly; and locking up removable disks, perhaps off-site. When actually using the computer, we should take care not to leave confidential information unattended on the screen. Similarly, we should protect hard copy, especially if it is spooled to a shared printer.

Development Process Issues

This book has already presented a number of examples involving an important ethical issue that relates to the development process: the issue of an incomplete or unreliable program that fails to do what is expected. Suppose a development team rushes a program to meet a deadline—perhaps to coincide with the introduction of a new product or to avoid the wrath of management. Or, maybe the team performs insufficient systems analysis. Or, perhaps the program was based on incomplete specifications.

Issues of systems development involve computer "professionals" who, because of their specialized knowledge, bear certain responsibilities. When they say a program is fully tested, they are believed because they are professionals. When they mislead, they violate professional ethics and damage the profession and themselves as individuals. A shoddy program can damage the client, as well.

Another ethical issue that relates to the development process is software piracy, the copying of copyrighted software. It is estimated that as much as 50 percent of all PC programs are pirated copies. The most common excuse for pirating software is that the individual or organization cannot afford to buy it and, without it, the person or firm will be at a disadvantage in the marketplace.

Issues Involving Managers and Subordinates

The area of systems development is where issues are likely to arise between managers and subordinates. In the information systems organization, there are multiple levels of authority and responsibility. These differing levels of personal power can lead to ethical dilemmas. Two examples follow.

- Because he feels he should have been promoted instead of someone else, a programmer plants a "bomb" program to destroy data he knows is important to the company.

- A manager demands that a programmer write an accounting routine that the programmer feels does not conform to generally accepted accounting principles.

Processing Issues

The category of processing issues includes three types of problems: problems of unreliability, problems of untimely output, and problems of unintended data use.

Problems of Unreliability

Ethical issues arising from the operation of computers are to a great extent issues of hardware and software *un*reliability and the failure to anticipate it. These dilemmas occur, in part, because of the increasing degree of application complexity, and the growing dependence of organizations and individuals on computers. As applications and the computers they run on get more complex, they are harder to test, fix, and operate without interruption or error. As people and organizations get more dependent on computers, they are more inconvenienced by not having them. If the system is down, harm may result. This could be as catastrophic as an airliner crash due to the failure of an air-controller's computer or as simple as a faulty ATM that forces a person in need of cash to seek another machine. In both cases, a promised service is not delivered and some harm results. Were there contingency plans? Did they work? If not, why not?

Problems of Untimely Output

As an example of an untimely output, consider the case of a late-clearing check. Who is responsible when this happens? What should or can be done about it?

Problems of Unintended Data Use

Another processing dilemma is how to prevent the unintended use of data. Data should not be collected for one purpose, then arbitrarily used for something else. For example, a bank should not, without the cardholders' knowledge, use information about credit-card purchases to create a consumer profile for marketing purposes. The key aspect of this issue is permission. The cardholders agreed to have information about their purchases recorded, but they did not give permission to be profiled and for that profile to be distributed to others. The practice of computer matching comes under this category—when, for example, the IRS compares its tapes with other agencies' tapes to catch parents who fail to pay child support.

Issues Relating to the Workplace

The two primary issues in this category are ergonomics and employee monitoring.

Ergonomics

The field of ergonomics relates to the physical work environment. The question is how far an organization should go to be "ergonomically sound"? For example, what is required to provide data entry clerks with a "healthful" work area? How can a firm create an environment that results in minimal eyestrain, guards against back problems, prevents repetitive-motion syndrome, and protects against CRT emissions?

Monitoring

Monitoring, in this context, means tracking and measuring employee activity. What are the ethics of using technology to keep track of employee performance? Items tracked might include number of keystrokes, error rate, and number of transactions processed. Is it ethical to monitor phone lines by computer to determine a caller's number, when he or she called, and how long the call lasted? Should a supervisor listen in on a call? Such monitoring systems are not necessarily illegal. The ethical questions include the following:

- Does the employee or caller know about the monitoring system?

- Does he or she understand how the information is to be used?

- Does he or she agree to its use?

Issues of Data Collection, Storage, and Access

These issues relate to the need to protect data confidentiality, privacy, and accuracy. How much data do you collect? Only what you need, or all you can get? Some reason that you ought to collect it now in case you need it in the future. Is this a justifiable position? For instance, should a human resources department collect and store police-record data about employees when there is no current need for that data? Is the data obtained with or without the permission or knowledge of the subject? Under what circumstances should you seek permission from or inform those whose records are on file?

How accurate is the data we collect? For that matter, how accurate does data need to be? For example, the quality of some marketing decisions might not be diminished by using sales data that was not totally accurate. On the other hand, there would be great potential for harm if a medical record was inaccurate.

How much effort should be made to correct errors? Is it feasible or necessary for a data file to be 100 percent accurate? Does the subject of the data have the opportunity to examine the file to detect and correct errors?

Who has access to the data? Who knows what persons have exercised access privileges? Who knows what persons have tried to exercise access privileges but failed because they were unauthorized? Should we keep logs of all successful and unsuccessful accesses? What effort has been made to protect the data from theft? How long do we keep data?

Who owns the data? Answering this will often resolve some of the earlier questions. Ownership implies certain rights and responsibilities. Usually, the owner is responsible for error detection and correction. But ownership needs to be defined and agreed upon by all parties; this is not an easy task.

Issues About Electronic Mail

This is a special category because of the increasing popularity of e-mail. The basis question: Is a user's privacy protected, as in the U.S. Mail, or does the owner of the e-mail system have the right to monitor system content? The issues of permission and informed consent are present here. Do the employees know that the e-mail is being read, and do they agree to that?

In addition, e-mail provides unique opportunities for the abuse of another's resource. For instance, it is quite easy to fill an e-mail network with extraneous messages. Simply sending personal messages without permission may be unethical.

Resource Exploitation Issues

This category includes wasting resources, interrupting services, and taking advantage of vulnerable systems. Some examples of resource exploitation follow.

- *Planting viruses:* Viruses are programs that reproduce themselves and destroy or alter other programs or data.

- *Hacking:* Hackers are people who plant viruses, break into computers to read files, steal data, and alter programs. Recently, some reformed hackers have offered their expertise in a consulting capacity to help firms protect against other hackers. This presents a special ethical dilemma: Should unethical practice be rewarded in this way?

- *Planting logic bombs:* Logic bombs are programs or pieces of programs that maliciously destroy data, other programs, or hardware. These bombs are often planted by disgruntled employees or political, social, or religious zealots who attempt to use the technology to achieve their own end.

- *Using an employer's computer for personal gain:* Some of the computer use in this category is "casual" and likened to taking pens and pads home from the office. But some employees have been discovered running outside personal businesses by using their employer's computer.

Vendor-Client Issues

This category encompasses all situations in which one party, the vendor, is supplying hardware, software, or a service to another party, the client. Vendor-client issues generally involve payment for services rendered. The vendor provides a service for a fee, and the client pays the fee and receives that service. The contract that binds the two parties implies or explicitly states the obligations of each party. Such contracts are becoming larger and more complex as the practice of outsourcing becomes prevalent. A company that outsources contracts with an outside agency, which will serve the company's computing needs. The agency could provide anything from development of a computer system to day-to-day computer operations.

Ethical issues in this category are usually related to nonperformance according to contract and disagreements over implied warranties. Suppose a vendor fails to deliver software by the promised date. Or, suppose the software is delivered but that it lacks the promised functionality. In one famous incident a firm decided that the programs a software vendor wrote did not work well enough. When the firm could get no satisfaction from the vendor, it held up further payment for the programs. Such withholding is a common business practice. But the software vendor had embedded a routine in several programs that would prevent them from being used if the firm stopped paying. The vendor activated the routine, and the firm could no longer use the programs. The firm's operations were severely affected. The vendor's position was that the product had been "repossessed" because of nonpayment.

Some other common examples of ethical dilemmas in client-vendor relations follow.

- To meet the advertised release date, a software development company ships a database management system to customers, even though it has not been fully tested.

- A user continually changes system specifications, resulting in delays and added expense to the developer. This situation can occur between a user and a systems analyst, who both work for the same firm. Though an outside vendor is not involved, the client-vendor relationship and the responsibility to act ethically still exist.

- A consultant sells a program to a second client after being paid to develop that software exclusively for the first client.

- A vendor provides hardware maintenance according to a written contract that calls for hardware to be repaired in a "timely manner." The client does not believe that repairs have been timely.

Issues of Computer Crime

This area involves using the computer as a tool to perform illegal acts—fraud, embezzlement, and the like. There are many reports of computer crime, but experts believe the number of crimes far outstrips the number of reports. Firms seem reluctant to report computer crimes. Managers are embarrassed that they let the crime happen, and they know that prosecuting perpetrators is difficult. However, the failure to prosecute does not in any way diminish the importance of computer crime or the size of the risk to individuals and firms from it. The incidence of computer crime is rising, as is the magnitude of the harm it generates.

One computer crime that is getting increasing attention is the use of imaging and desktop publishing technology to create, copy, or alter official documents. What this shows is that technological change spawns ever-changing threats.

SUMMARY

Because computers permeate our work and personal lives, all of us have an obligation to see that they are used responsibly. The factors that characterize ethical dilemmas in a computer environment include the speed of a computer, vulnerability of computer data to unauthorized change, and the fact that protecting information often decreases its accessibility. Because of the order-of-magnitude effect, harmless situations may turn into harmful ones without our realizing it. The elimination of the effort required to access and collate large quantities of data poses its own threat.

The social implications of information technology include such issues as job displacement, power, and access. As individuals, we have the responsibility to protect resources and confidentiality by employing sound computer practices. Other ethical issues relate to systems development; manager-subordinate relations; computer processing; workplace design and practices; data collection, storage, and access; e-mail; misuse of another's resources; vendor-client relations; and crime.

REFERENCES

Axline, Larry, and Mark Pastin. The high-ethics manager, *Information Executive*, Fall 1989, 21–25, 61.

Bologna, Jack. Ethical issues of the information era, *Computers & Security*, September 1990, 689–692.

Gellerman, Saul W. Managing ethics from the top down, *Information Executive*, Fall 1989, 27–30, 32–33.

Gentile, Mary, and John J. Sviokla. Information technology in organizations: Emerging issues in ethics and policy, *Harvard Business School* 9–190–130, February 15, 1990.

Mason, Richard O. Four ethical issues of the information age, *MIS Quarterly*, March 1986, 5–12.

Parker, Donn B. Ethics for information systems personnel, *Journal of Information Systems Management*, Summer 1988, 44–48.

Parker, D., S. Swope, and B. Baker. *Ethical Conflicts in Information and Computer Science, Technology, and Business*, Wellesley, MA: QED Information Sciences, 1990.

Rifkin, Glenn. The ethics gap, *Computerworld* (Executive Report), October 14, 1991, 83–90.

CHAPTER 3

Solving Ethical Dilemmas
A Sample Case Exercise

A FOUR-STEP ANALYSIS PROCESS

In chapter 1, you learned how to make defensible ethical decisions. The term *defensible* is important in this context. Although the emotions play an important role in the decision-making process, you have learned that defensible decisions are those that have been made by considering objective guidelines, both formal and informal. This process of logical analysis does more than help resolve a current dilemma; the analysis can help prevent or solve similar problems in the future.

In this chapter, you will employ the techniques you learned in Chapter 1 and expand on them. You will learn to recognize the relevant facts before you make an ethical decision, and you will see how to implement a decision and apply the fruits of your analysis to prevent the problem from recurring. The means to these skills is a four-step process that this chapter will present along with a case study. Step II of the process contains the decision-making method you learned in Chapter 1; other parts of the process will be new to you.

This chapter will apply the four-step process to the case study and provide extensive commentary. As you work through the steps, you may well be surprised at how many levels ethical problems contain. As soon as one layer is "peeled" away, another appears. As ethical problem solvers, we must be sure we have exposed all the layers before implementing a decision; terminating analysis too soon may lead to a poor conclusion. The best way to ensure consideration of all aspects is to conscientiously complete the entire four-step process.

To begin your study of the four-step analysis process, read the steps in their entirety. The whole process is stated in the outline that follows; parts of the outline will be repeated later in the chapter.

Step I   Analyze the situation. What is the subject of this case? What is it all about?
   A.   What are the relevant facts?
   B.   Who are the stakeholders—that is, who has an interest, or stake, in the outcome?

Step II   Make a defensible ethical decision. (Refer to Chapter 1 for details.)
   A.   Isolate the ethical issues.
      1.   Should someone have done or not done something?
      2.   Does it matter that . . . ? (reasons and excuses)
   B.   Examine the legal issues.
   C.   Consult guidelines.
      1.   Do corporate policies apply?
      2.   What codes of conduct apply?
      3.   Does the action violate the Golden Rule?
      4.   Who benefits? Who is harmed?
      5.   Does the action pass tests for right and wrong?
   D.   Discover the applicable ethical principles.
      1.   Explore ways to minimize harm.
      2.   Analyze pertinent rights and duties.
      3.   Define professional responsibilities.
      4.   Examine the situation in terms of egoism and utilitarianism.
      5.   Apply concepts of consistency and respect.
   E.   Make a defensible choice.

Step III   Describe steps to resolve the current situation.
   A.   What are the options at this time?
   B.   Which option(s) do you recommend?

C.   Defend the legality and ethicality of your recommenda-
     tion.
D.   How would you implement your recommendation?
E.   Recommend short-term corrective measures.
     1.   Analyze the pivot points.
     2.   Alter the parameters.

Step IV   Prepare policies and strategies to prevent recurrence.
A.   What organizational, political, legal, technological, or so-
     cietal changes are needed?
B.   What are the consequences of your suggested changes?
     1.   What happens when this resolution is invoked?
     2.   What obstacles might prevent your plan from work-
          ing?
     3.   Why should the organization implement the
          changes?
     4.   How do the changes benefit the organization? Are
          they marketable, or do they further public relations?
          (Perhaps perform a cost-benefit analysis.)
     5.   Do the changes increase the net good for those con-
          cerned? Does anyone get hurt?
     6.   Do the changes support human rights and reflect
          common duties?

SAMPLE CASE: TOO MUCH OF A GOOD THING?

Clare Valerian is a systems analyst at Califon, Inc., a large distributor of electronic equipment. Her primary responsibility is to make certain that the 127
end-users in Califon's U.S. headquarters can access data, post to accounts,
send and receive e-mail, and accomplish all the other duties they need to perform on the corporation's local area network. She describes herself as a facil-
itator and troubleshooter. She must respond quickly to the users' complaints
and needs, and even provide training for novice users. It's a demanding and
time-consuming job, and until two weeks ago, Clare was spending up to 12
hours a day one-on-one with her users. She spent much of her time traveling
to various sites in the different corporate buildings. The telephone was not

much help, because Clare had to see for herself exactly what the users saw on their screens. Now, however, a utility program called LANSCAPE has changed her workday completely. The utility program and the telephone at her desk allow her to solve user problems without ever having to go directly to the users' workstations and terminals. The program allows Clare to view and actually take over the activities of network users. Typically, her first task upon arriving at her desk is to check her e-mail messages for trouble spots, print the messages out, fire up LANSCAPE, and call each user one at a time.

"John, this is Clare in Systems. You left me a message about a problem with the inventory reorder module. I've got your screen up on my terminal now. Can you get out of the word processor and transfer to the inventory system? . . . Good, I see the main menu. . . . Now, the reorder module. Go ahead and repeat the steps that got you into trouble yesterday. . . . OK, fine . . . oops, I see what you did. They system asks for ENTER and you hit RETURN. What kind of keyboard do you have? . . . That's what I thought. For now, remember to hit ENTER. I'll get the maintenance programmer to change the module to accept RETURN too. Sorry about that. . . . Thanks, good-bye.

Then Clare goes on to the next call. "Bill, this is Clare in Systems. Your word processor bombed? Why don't you call it up and repeat the . . . Oh, I see the problem. You're working with the buggy version, 2.3. I'll delete it from the system. You'll have to remember to use V2.4 from now on. . . . No problem. Good-bye.

Clare is delighted with the LANSCAPE utility. She roves electronically from one troubled user to another, seeing on her screen exactly what the user sees. The amount of time it takes to solve the problems is about the same, but because she can solve them from her desk, she has eliminated the frustrating delays of travel time. She is at her desk when the users call, and they are pleased with the fast response time.

Clare even has time to scan users' activities without their making a request. Her troubleshooting has become more proactive than reactive. She can scan a number of users without their knowledge, and when she finds one in trouble can interrupt and help.

"Harry, this is Clare in Systems. I'm looking at your screen now. . . . I know you didn't call, but I thought I'd beat you to the punch. You can speed up that multiple posting to a single customer by using the TAB key instead of updating the record for each entry. . . . Yes, like that. . . . Glad to be of service."

Last week Clare and her boss, the director of user support, met with the vice president of information systems, Art Betony, to evaluate LANSCAPE. Clare said, "Without this program, I'd have to control the activities of every user in every system test and move from one building to the other. With LANSCAPE, I can watch over their shoulders without being there. LANSCAPE is inexpensive and easy to use. I fully endorse its continued use and recommend we obtain additional copies and make it available to all support personnel." The three went on to discuss the increase in user satisfaction and productivity that had resulted from the use of LANSCAPE.

Yesterday Art was having his usual Tuesday lunch with his boss, Executive Vice President Alberta Wilson. Art couldn't stop praising the LANSCAPE.

Alberta seemed especially interested. "You mean you can tell me at any time what people are doing?"

"Not quite," Art answered. "We can only see the screens of the users who are logged in. But of course that's exactly what my people need for their purposes."

"But the people you observe this way . . . do they know their screens are being observed?"

"No, not unless we tell them. The LANSCAPE program doesn't change anything on their screens. Of course, that's a necessary feature of the system, because my people have to see exactly what the users see."

"Could you install LANSCAPE on my terminal, in my office?"

"Of course. But what value would that be?"

Alberta leaned forward and whispered. "I shouldn't reveal this outside the Human Resources Department, but I think I will to enlist your support. Here at headquarters, we may have one or more persons dealing in drugs. We have suspects but no proof. Somehow these people are taking orders and making deliveries right on the premises, during company time. I suspect they are using the phone and maybe even the computer to make their deals. We have tried various surveillance methods to no avail. What I want to do is use LANSCAPE to randomly check on what the suspects are doing. Then, if we catch them red-handed, we'll have our evidence and we can prosecute."

Art frowned and said, "Gee, I don't know if I should give you that software, Alberta. Let me think about it and get back to you."

CASE COMMENTARY

This commentary will follow the four-step analysis process to reach a conclusion about the sample case. Sometimes the responses to the four-step process are specific and apply directly to one of the questions in the steps. At other times the comments are more general. The kind of answer depends, to a large extent, on the facts available and the details of the situation.

> **Step I**   Analyze the situation. What is the subject of this case? What is it all about?
>   A. What are the relevant facts?
>   B. Who are the stakeholders—that is, who has an interest, or stake, in the outcome?

Begin by reviewing step I.

Step I may seem simplistic and unnecessary. Yet great confusion and wasted effort can result if all do not understand the situation in the same way and agree on the facts. It need not take long, but step I is essential.

The case study presents many facts. Some are more relevant than others. The stating of the facts should be, as much as possible, a neutral, logical exercise. Although interpretation is involved in selecting pertinent facts, do not judge them in this step. Comments such as "Clare should not have viewed anyone's screen without their permission" are inappropriate in this step. The fact that Clare "roves electronically," however, must be noted. Rightness or wrongness will be discussed in step II.

What Are the Relevant Facts?

The list that follows presents the pertinent facts:

- Califon is a distributor of electronic equipment, with a large in-house computer system supporting more than 100 users.

- Clare Valerian is a Califon tech-support person who helps end-users with their computer problems.

- Clare has a new utility program, LANSCAPE, that enables her to duplicate on her screen exactly what is taking place on a user's screen.

- LANSCAPE allows someone to observe another's computer activity without his or her knowledge.

- LANSCAPE enables Clare to avoid having to go to the user to solve a problem, resulting in greater efficiency and more satisfied users.

- Clare not only responds to requests for help but also "roves electronically," viewing, without their permission, what people are doing.

- Clare makes suggestions to the users, even when she has not received a help call from them.

- Clare recommends continued use of LANSCAPE and suggests making it available to others in her group who perform similar troubleshooting activities.

- Art Betony, V.P. for Information Systems, is so impressed with LANSCAPE that he tells of its success to Alberta Wilson, Califon executive V.P.

- Alberta reveals that there may be a drug-dealing operation at Califon.

- Alberta admits to other surveillance attempts.

- Alberta asks Art to install LANSCAPE on her terminal so she can monitor the computer activities of the suspected drug dealers.

- Art Betony makes no immediate commitment.

There may be other "facts" that could be added, such as the Califon chain of command. Or, it may be argued that some of the "facts" listed are really value judgments or opinions and should be deleted in favor of purely objective statements. For example, the statement that Clare was "roving electronically" without permission is in one sense a fact from the case, but it is in another sense a judgment about Clare's actions. Thus, an argument could be made to leave it off the list in step I. If you take that position, be sure Clare's rovings are included in the discussion in step II.

The best approach for the sake of completeness is to list *all* facts in step I, even if you will refer to some of them again in step II. If it makes sense to distinguish "subjective" facts and "objective" facts, label them appropriately. Of course the two primary questions in this step—What is the subject of this case? and What is it all about?—have a variety of answers. The answers to these questions should be simple. Longer answers tend to bring in the reasons for the actions, and they belong in step II. In this case, the answers must reflect the fact that LANSCAPE allows one person to monitor what others are doing at their computers without their knowledge, that LANSCAPE is a useful tool for technical-support personnel, that the executive V.P. thinks there is drug dealing at Califon, and that the executive V.P. says she wants to use LANSCAPE to monitor employee computer use to find the drug dealers.

Who Are the Stakeholders?

The listing of stakeholders is a key task in this analysis because it helps to determine who is affected by the action. Often there are some surprises from this part of the exercise. Sometimes just realizing that someone is a stakeholder influences the solution and recommendations. In this case, stakeholders include:

Clare
The director of user support
Art Betony, V.P., Information Systems
Alberta Wilson, executive V.P.
The other tech-support people
All computer users at Califon
The suspected drug dealers
The drug users, the customers of the dealers
Califon as a whole
All Califon employees
Califon stockholders
Califon customers
Society as a whole
The producers of LANSCAPE
Other LANSCAPE users

A judgment must be made whether a stakeholder is important enough to be listed. There may be a number of secondary, or fringe, stakeholders, and including them and their claims might not contribute much to the solution. For instance, in this case other users of LANSCAPE could be stakeholders because any misuse of that software or bad publicity it gets might have implications for them. But such an occurrence, should it happen, is clearly not central to the issue. Fringe stakeholders might be listed for the sake of thoroughness or as a way of accounting for all concerned parties. But it is a waste of time to spend any further effort on those whose interests have no significant bearing on the outcomes.

Step II   Make a defensible ethical decision. (Refer to Chapter 1 for details.)

A.   Isolate the ethical issues.
  1.   Should someone have done or not done something?
  2.   Does it matter that . . . ? (reasons and excuses)

B.   Examine the legal issues.

C.   Consult guidelines.
  1.   Do corporate policies apply?
  2.   What codes of conduct apply?
  3.   Does the action violate the Golden Rule?

4. Who benefits? Who is harmed?
5. Does the action pass tests for right and wrong?
D. Discover the applicable ethical principles.
    1. Explore ways to minimize harm.
    2. Analyze pertinent rights and duties.
    3. Define professional responsibilities.
    4. Examine the situation in terms of egoism and utilitarianism.
    5. Apply concepts of consistency and respect.
E. Make a defensible choice.

The task in step II is to see clearly the consequences or the implications of each of the actions and to recognize who is affected and to what extent. Only then can you explore the reasons for the actions and determine whether they can be supported. This is where you apply the ethical guidelines and principles discussed in Chapter 1. It is critical to discover the guidelines or principles that apply so you can become sensitized to situations that may be unethical. By doing so, you will learn to generalize appropriate behavior to similar situations.

Isolate the Ethical Issues

First, it is essential to isolate the major ethical issues.
Consider these questions:

Should . . .

. . . Art Betony provide Alberta Wilson with LANSCAPE so she can monitor activity?

. . . Alberta Wilson monitor employee computer use without the employees' knowledge or consent?

. . . Clare have been more explicit in telling her users that she could observe them without their knowledge?

. . . Clare have done her electronic roving without the knowledge and consent of her users?

. . . Califon management have established a policy on computer monitoring prior to implementing LANSCAPE?

. . . Alberta have told Art Betony about the suspected drug dealing?

. . . Art refuse the request of his superior?

Some of these issues are more important than others. One position is that monitoring without knowledge or permission is the most serious issue. But the minor issues should not be overlooked, because they often provide insights into attitudes or actions that contribute to solutions.

In addition, it is important to evaluate all the reasons that the actors give or may give to justify their actions. One way to do this is to ask the question Does it matter that . . . ? and then add each of the reasons in turn. You should be able to differentiate between weak excuses and reasonable mitigating circumstances.

The actors' rationales in this case include the following:

Does it matter that . . .

. . . the culprits were committing a serious crime, dealing drugs, rather than some minor offense?

. . . the producers of LANSCAPE may have had no intention of their program being used in this way?

. . . Califon had no policy on computer monitoring?

. . . LANSCAPE produced enormous productivity gains?

. . . Alberta had previously sanctioned other forms of surveillance?

. . . the surveillance utility was specifically designed so the user would be unaware of its operation?

Having established one or more issues, there are many ways to apply ethical guidelines to the situation. Some decision makers prefer a free-form approach, where observations arise randomly through interaction with the other participants. Ultimately, however, the discussant should list the arguments and their ethical principles in an orderly fashion and make some attempt at consensus. The approach based on the process outlined in Chapter 1 is structured. In this process the first step in making a defensible ethical decision is to examine existing laws.

Examine the Legal Issues

There are four possible conditions:

- Ethical and legal

- Ethical but not legal

- Not ethical but legal
- Not ethical and not legal

The illegality of the drug dealing is not in question. The main legal issue is whether monitoring is permitted. Generally, under current law, it is not illegal to monitor employee activity. Recent legislative efforts in some states require official notification of employees. Employers must tell them (1) they are being monitored, (2) what information is being collected, and (3) what it is to be used for. Assuming that no legislation exists, nothing illegal would take place if Alberta got her way. That eliminates conditions of illegality. Thus, the question is now whether the proposed act is ethical or unethical. The law does not give us a clear direction. The next course is to consult some guidelines to obtain further insight.

Consult Guidelines

Is the act consistent with corporate policy? We are not told of any corporate policy about monitoring. Art Betony should find out if there is one. Based on the fact of prior surveillance, whose form we are not made aware of, there may be a policy allowing monitoring. But the likelihood is that there is no policy at all about monitoring. It is not unusual for even large organizations to have few explicit policies, especially concerning computer use. And often, when there are policies, they are not well publicized or enforced. In this case we lack knowledge of any policies, so we must assume none exist.

This lack of information about whether there are policies is not a weakness in this sample case. This condition is deliberately included to show that decision makers never have all the information they want. Sometimes they can afford to spend the time and other resources to find out more. But, at some point, they must make decisions based on whatever information they have on hand.

A second general guideline asks whether the act violates corporate or professional codes of conduct. Though other codes exist, we will use the ACM Code of Ethics and Professional Conduct as the reference (see Chapter 1). Some imperatives that might apply are:

1. *General Moral Imperatives*
   As an ACM member I will . . .

   1.1 Contribute to society and human well-being

Apprehending the drug dealers will certainly contribute to society. This imperative supports giving LANSCAPE to the executive V.P.

1.2 Avoid harm to others

Computer users who are not involved with drugs may be harmed if they are monitored. Their privacy might be violated. Personal messages, if they are permitted, may be revealed. Also, their actions may be subject to misinterpretation, as explained later in the discussion of the Golden Rule. So, on that basis, Art should avoid participation in the monitoring. On the other hand, anyone seduced into drug use is surely being harmed; so stopping the drug dealing would reduce or eliminate that effect. From that standpoint, facilitating the monitoring might be ethically defensible.

1.8 Respect the privacy of others

As stated above, innocent computer users, as well as the guilty, have their privacy violated by the monitoring.

3. Organizational Leadership Imperatives
As an ACM member and an organizational leader, I will . . .

3.2 Manage personnel and resources to design and build information systems that enhance the quality of working life

Monitoring without knowledge and permission, it may be argued, does not enhance the quality of working life of those monitored. Sooner or later, facts or even rumors about the monitoring will surface. The outcome could include any number of results, fear and resentment among them.

3.3 Acknowledge and support proper and authorized uses of an organization's computing and communication resources

This imperative summarizes Art Betony's dilemma. Is the monitoring a proper and authorized use of the computing resource? If there is a policy that allows it, the monitoring may be authorized. But that is only half the requirement; the use must also be proper. But the code is not helpful in labeling this action as proper or improper.

3.5 Articulate and support policies that protect the dignity of users and others affected by a computing system

It could be argued that monitoring without permission or knowledge does not protect dignity or that it is an action that shows disrespect for the individual. Using this point of view, Article 3.5 would support Art in not providing the software to Alberta Wilson.

In summary, reference to the ACM code leaves us with the ethical problem unsolved. There is a strong argument in favor of monitoring—to foster human well-being. But there are some imperatives that support respecting privacy, the opposing view. Finally, there are imperatives such as 3.3, which represent a worthwhile objective but do not contribute to the solution directly.

The next guideline asks Does the action violate the Golden Rule? In other words, would we want this to be done to us? Would we want our work monitored without our knowledge or permission? Some might answer that they have nothing to hide, so such monitoring would be OK. Others might argue that they have nothing to hide but that, since some actions are open to interpretation, they would object to monitoring. For instance, suppose the person being monitored is creating a word processing document. The observer might monitor that activity and see that hardly any words are being keyed and conclude that the worker is lazy or inefficient. The worker, however, is actually composing a major market analysis and consulting numerous source documents. Thus, research time is interspersed with the typing. In the Califon case, it appears that the Golden Rule does not give us a conclusive answer.

The fourth guideline questions whether the act serves a majority, a minority, or just one person. In this case the majority would be served if the drug dealers could be caught. Only a few would be monitored, some of whom would be innocent; and all stakeholders would benefit from apprehension of the culprits. Though Alberta would receive praise for a job well done, her motive for doing this does not appear to be self-serving; she seems simply to be executing a job responsibility.

The tests for rightness and wrongness provide no clear-cut direction either. Applying the Mom Test, we might easily say we'd be happy to tell our moms about how we apprehended the drug dealers. But we might not want to tell how we invaded some innocent people's privacy. As for the TV Test, we probably would not want any nationwide publicity about the drug dealing. But, if the perpetrators were apprehended, that might make a difference. As for going public about the monitoring itself, the effect of doing so might depend on how the story was told. The Smell Test is also inconclusive. Things don't "smell" great, but they are not awful either. The monitoring might not be absolutely good but it is being used to do a good thing, catch a crook. The Other Person's Shoes Test, in this case, brings a conclusion similar to examination of the case in terms of the Golden Rule. Finally, the Market Test is not helpful, since Califon would not get any marketing benefit from any of the circumstances. This leads us to an examination of ethical principles.

Discover the Applicable Ethical Principles

The principles involved in this case follow.

- The users have a *right* to know that they could be secretly monitored.

- The users have a *right* to the privacy of their workplace.

- Califon has the *right* to protect its computer resource and its business from misuse and abuse.

- Alberta has a *right* to expect Art, her subordinate, to carry out her orders if they are not illegal or immoral.

- Clare has a *duty* to explain the monitoring function of LANSCAPE to users. This is an issue of *trust*, *integrity*, and *truthfulness* emanating from her *professional relationship* with the users. She, as the professional, has superior knowledge and the *responsibility* to see that those without it are not *harmed*.

- Art has a *duty* to carry out orders from his superior, Alberta.

- To ensure *minimum harm* and the *greatest public welfare* and as a result of the principle of *efficacy*, Art has a *duty* to advise Alberta of all the factors involved in using LANSCAPE.

- Clare's act of "roving electronically" and observing clients without their requesting it may be a form of *self-interest* if she understood the privacy violation but felt that she would gain (in terms of praise and promotion) from the "better" job she was doing.

- From a *utilitarian* point of view, society and Califon would be much better off without drug dealers. Therefore, the "small" privacy violation would be greatly outweighed by the improvement in the public good, assuming the dealers were caught.

- Kant's *principle of consistency* argues against the monitoring of suspected drug dealers, since we would not want everyone to be monitored or everyone to be able to monitor another at will.

- Monitoring without knowledge or permission violates Kant's *principle of respect*. Those monitored are being treated as means rather than ends.

Make a Defensible Choice

After listing and discussing arguments and principles, it is necessary to weigh them and draw conclusions. In this case, the issue boils down to user privacy rights versus the public good of apprehending drug dealers and the corporate good of the intrinsic value of LANSCAPE. The better argument is that the right to privacy and the issues of permission and informed consent outweigh the consequence of discovering the drug dealers. In some circumstances, rights may legitimately be set aside or limited, especially when other rights may be at stake. For instance, invasions of privacy may be justified to prevent greater harm, such as breaking into a locked dorm room when smoke is discovered coming under the door. The need to put out the fire, and perhaps save a life, overrides the privacy right. Based on what we know in this case, it is not clear whether preventing the greater harm (drug dealing) will really be achieved. We have no idea of the extent of the drug operation, how much harm it is doing, how much risk of harm Califon and its employees have, how sure Alberta is that the drug dealing exists, what chance she has of actually finding the culprit, how admissible the evidence acquired from the monitoring will be, how many people she suspects, how strong her suspicions are, what the law enforcement authorities have to do with this, what the opinions of the CEO and Board of Directors are or whether they have been informed at all.

Furthermore, we have no idea of what harm will be caused to innocent people who are included in the monitoring. Nor do we know whether such monitoring will stop after the drug bust. Suppose the culprits are really dealing drugs but are not using the computer to help them. How far and for how long would the search be expanded before this is discovered?

It makes no difference that Alberta previously performed other forms of surveillance. Those actions may have been illegal and unethical. It also makes no difference that Art is Alberta's subordinate. His duty to the organization and other stakeholders overrides his relationship with Alberta. Of course, as a practical matter, he may lose his job or suffer other harm that has implications for his duty to self and family. But that is insufficient reason for him to violate his responsibility as a computer professional and act unethically. Thus, Art should refuse to allow Alberta to use LANSCAPE as she proposes.

In addition, there may be other remedies to this situation that do not present the need to act unethically (see step III). Step II, making an ethical decision, may leave us feeling uncomfortable. Perhaps because we have not tied up all the loose ends or maybe some harm results from the choice we make, even though it appears the best choice possible. Ethical choices are not made with absolute certainty; they are not deductive like mathematical problems and solutions. Ethical decisions are made through judgment and by validating judgment through a rational appeal to principles. The danger is in not acting at all, in not ever making a decision or judgment. Failing to act will simply allow a wrongful situation to continue or get worse. As the axiom says, "Not to act, is to act." The best you can do is be aware of the opposing positions; make the decision on the available facts; and, as facts and circumstances change, have the courage to defend or change your decision.

Step II takes the most time and discussion. This is appropriate, since without fully understanding the ethical issues a quality decision cannot be achieved. However, developing the short- and long-term resolutions (steps III and IV) is essential for placing the situation in a real context, for moving from principles to practices.

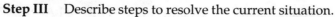

> **Step III**   Describe steps to resolve the current situation.
> A. What are the options at this time?
> B. Which option(s) do you recommend?
> C. Defend the legality and ethicality of your recommendation.
> D. How would you implement your recommendation?
> E. Recommend short-term corrective measures.
>   1. Analyze the pivot points.
>   2. Alter the parameters.

Both steps III and IV require realistic and practical solutions. Struggling to achieve them gives insight into the complexity of the problem under discussion. Step III asks what, as a manager or as one of the actors, you can do now.

What Are the Options at This Time?

Based on the facts in this case, the major options are to give Alberta what she wants or deny her request.

Which Options Do You Recommend?

Art and Alberta might decide to involve top management, perhaps even the Board of Directors. They must get answers to the questions raised in step II: Is there a policy governing monitoring? What previous type of surveillance has taken place? Who knew about it? Was it legal? Did law enforcement authorities get involved? Just how serious is the risk to Califon? How many people are involved? What is the basis of the suspicion of drug dealing? What is the likelihood of discovering sufficient evidence for arrest and conviction? These answers will put the problem in better perspective and may lead to further questions and suggestions for action.

Defend the Legality and Ethicality of Your Recommendation

At the very least, a top-level policy decision on monitoring should result. Such a policy might state that the computer resource is owned by Califon and is to be used for Califon business. Further, it could state that no presumption of privacy should be made by those using the system. As an example or as a special section, the use and *full* capability of LANSCAPE could be explained.

How Would You Implement Your Recommendation?

Publishing the policy would put all users on notice, would satisfy the knowledge requirement, and might ethically justify some limited monitoring to dis-cover the drug dealers. The drug dealers could react in two ways. They could take the publication of the policy casually, as just another memo to be filed. In that case, they might well be caught through the monitoring. Or, if they took the memo seriously, they would stop using the computer for their activities. This might diminish or end their ability to operate at Califon or force them to operate in a more open manner that leads to their discovery. In other words, being open and ethical about the potential for monitoring might very well have the same result as being covert and unethical.

Recommend Short-Term Corrective Measures

Sometimes there is not much that can be done immediately. This is typical when the unethical act has already taken place. But one way to discover corrective measures is to try to find the pivot points in the scenario. Where could the situation have "turned around" if only someone has done something differently? In this case, one pivot point was when the decision was made to perform the original surveillance. A policy decision was needed then, and it would have helped with the LANSCAPE problem. A policy is needed now.

A second pivot point was when LANSCAPE was first purchased and used. There was no ethical impact study or any consideration of how it was to be used. Had that happened, Clare may not have been free to rove, users may have been more explicitly informed, and Alberta's request may never have arisen. So, a second immediate recommendation is to undertake an ethical analysis whenever new software is to be used. Identifying pivot points is valuable for sensitizing individuals to the early-warning signs of an ethical situation. The earlier an ethical dilemma is discovered, the easier it is to solve, since there will be fewer layers to the problem.

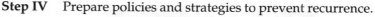

> **Step IV**   Prepare policies and strategies to prevent recurrence.
>   A.   What organizational, political, legal, technological, or societal changes are needed?
>   B.   What are the consequences of your suggested changes?
>   1.   What happens when this resolution is invoked?
>   2.   What obstacles might prevent your plan from working?
>   3.   Why should the organization implement the changes?
>   4.   How do the changes benefit the organization? Are they marketable, or do they further public relations? (Perhaps perform a cost-benefit analysis.)
>   5.   Do the changes increase the net good for those concerned? Does anyone get hurt?
>   6.   Do the changes support human rights and reflect duties?

Sometimes in step III or after step IV, it is worthwhile to alter some of the parameters in the case to see if different circumstances change the analysis and lead to different outcomes. This is useful in discovering variables that might be controllable and hence could be part of the short- and long-term solutions.

The following questions display one approach for altering parameters:

- Does it make a difference that Califon was an electronics company and not in some other industry?

- Does it make a difference that Alberta is a woman?

- What might have happened if one of the users had objected to Clare's observing without permission and had complained to another manager?

- What might have happened if Clare, in her roving, had discovered some improper computer use—game playing, for instance, or even the drug dealing?

- Does it make a difference that the offense is drug dealing and not something like game playing?

One question that should always be included is: If you could do it all over again, what would you do? In this case, one response to that question might be:

Califon should have had some sort of corporate antidrug campaign and policy that might have prevented the necessity for any of this. If the company had been vigilant early on, the dealing may never have started.

Step IV asks you to apply your knowledge of organizations, politics, the legislative process, technology, and society to suggest global, long-term solutions to prevent this kind of situation from happening again. You might also consider:

- What organization support structures or obstacles exist, and what might be needed?

- Can (additional) disclosure, communication, or compromise resolve the issue or prevent recurrence? How can this be done?

In this case, some suggestions are to:

- Foster an ethical corporate culture at Califon so that people such as Clare, Art, and Alberta can become sensitive to ethical situations.

- Develop a code of ethics, teach it, and reward it. Such an initiative often benefits the company in the form of a good reputation that is marketable.

- Establish an ethics hot line at Califon, an 800 number or some anonymous way of reporting unethical activity. This should include any unethical activity, not just unethical activities involving computers. Through such a vehicle Clare's roving might have been reported and the drug dealers might even have been exposed.

- Enact state or federal statutes to protect workers who are monitored. However, legal solutions often require a long time and great expense.

Each of these suggestions requires further discussion and analysis. This could amount to a comprehensive feasibility study that might include gathering more data about the proposed activity, performing a cost-benefit analysis, preparing an ethical impact statement, and drafting an implementation plan.

SUMMARY

As demonstrated through the analysis of the sample case, ethical problems comprise many layers. To make and implement sound ethical decisions, you must understand all the facts. The stronger positions are those supported by ethical principles. Short- and long-term resolutions are not easy to develop or implement.

You are now ready to solve cases and make ethically defensible decisions on your own—that is, you have the knowledge to give principled reasons for the decisions your reach.

THE CASES

The real-life cases presented in Part II reflect a variety of computer-related circumstances that call for ethical decision making. Many are based on the experiences of information systems professionals; others are based on the authors' own experiences and research.

Each case contains a number of factors. There are often multiple ethical issues, overlapping situations, and different personalities. And, as in real life, there are confounding circumstances and extraneous facts that must be weeded out.

After using the process recommended in Chapter 3 to read and discuss a number of cases, you should be able to:

- Distinguish the relevant facts of a case and discover the stakeholders—that is, those who have an interest, or stake, in the outcome.

- Discover the ethical issues, identify the ethical principles involved, and make a defensible ethical decision.

- Suggest alternate courses of action to resolve the current situation.

- Recommend long-term systemic, organizational, or societal policies and strategies to prevent a similar situation in the future.

Levity or Libel?
An E-Mail Based Effort to Boost Morale Backfires

The LowRider Tractor Corporation had a reputation for manufacturing heavy-duty earth-moving equipment. Its Military Division produced more tank turrets, hulls, and suspensions than any other contractor. For many years the Military Division sustained the corporation by its aggressive marketing of military hardware overseas. During the late 1980s and early 1990s, however, the Military Division decreased its orders for tank parts. Because LowRider was so dependent on tank hardware revenues, management was faced with the task of significantly reducing the workforce.

The Board of Directors of LowRider had never experienced such tough economic times. The directors issued a directive, which they called a reorganization, to reduce the payroll in each division by 10 percent over a six-month period. The severity and speed of the cut left little room for compromise. In some departments, workers were laid off without consideration of the value or length of their service at LowRider. The drastic downsizing was certain to cause resentment and ill will.

At LowRider's world headquarters in New Hope, Nebraska, Bill Brundle worked as a software engineer. He designed and installed graphics modeling programs. His department had suffered its share of cuts, and it seemed to everyone that the workload was greater than ever. Employee morale was at an all-time low.

In Bill's eyes, what his department needed was a good laugh, preferably at the company's expense. Maybe that would boost morale. He approached the department's test data designer, Betty Hastings, who was his closest friend and confidante. He told her about his idea for distributing a document that would be good for a laugh. Betty thought it was a grand idea and even offered to help, but he said he preferred to work alone.

Bill spent an entire evening at his terminal, composing a memo mocking the "reorganization." This memo poked fun at the upper levels of management and contained some four-letter words that, although common enough in motion pictures, are not used in polite society. After composing the memo, and signing it "Management," Bill distributed it through e-mail to all workers in the department.

The effect of the memo was immediate. Several people in Bill's department e-mailed it to other departments, and it traveled throughout the company. It was the sole topic of conversation at all gatherings. People laughed at some phrasings and wandered from one office to another to share discovered double meanings. Even the two sour-grapes guys who worked with Bill had a good laugh. A few workers blushed at some of the words, and some said, "I just don't find it at all funny." Bill sensed success. When asked who wrote it, however, he said, "I don't know." Betty also said nothing, though of course she knew who had written it. The memo was reprinted and copied, and it continued to spread like warm butter on hot toast.

Eventually, the division director, Harriet Corrigan, got a copy. Harriet didn't like the memo at all. It was difficult enough to reduce the size of the division without what she called "this kind of insensitive criticism."

Harriet promptly ordered technicians to identify the workstation from which the memo originated. They had no difficulty identifying the source. Bill was fired. But because Bill's job was crucial to the division, Harriet was obliged to replace him immediately. Betty Hastings replaced Bill the next day. This was fortunate for Betty, because her position as test data designer had been eliminated by the reorganization.

CASE WORKSHEET

(See Chapter 3 for details about how to carry out each step of the analysis.)

I.   Find the facts
     A.   List the relevant facts _____
          _____
          _____
          _____
          _____
          _____
          _____
          _____

     B.   List the stakeholders _____
          _____
          _____
          _____
          _____

II. Make a defensible ethical decision
     A.   Isolate the ethical issues (Should someone have done or not done something?)
          _____
          _____
          _____

     B.   Examine the legal issues _____
     C.   Consult guidelines
          Corporate policies, codes of conduct _____
          _____

          Golden Rule _____
          _____
          _____

          Who benefits? Who is harmed? _____
          _____
          _____

          Tests for right and wrong _____
          _____
          _____

D. Discover the applicable ethical principles
    Least harm _____

    _____

    Rights and duties _____

    _____

    Professional responsibilities _____

    _____

    Self-interest and utilitarianism _____

    _____

    Consistency and respect _____

    _____

E. Make a defensible choice _____

    _____

III. Describe steps to resolve the current situation
    A. Options _____

        _____

    B. Recommendation _____

        _____

        _____

    C. Defense _____

        _____

    D. Implementation _____

        _____

    E. Short-term corrective measures _____

        _____

IV. Prepare policies and strategies to prevent recurrence
    A. Describe the organizational, political, legal, technological, or societal changes needed _____

        _____

        _____

    B. Describe the consequences of your suggested changes _____

        _____

        _____

Credit Woes
A Credit Bureau Faces a Decision
of Whether to Revise a System

Annabelle and Arvin Dorland made an offer on a three-bedroom house in Grande Pointe, New Hampshire. The sellers accepted the offer, and everything seemed to be going well. The home was their dream house, with all the features they ever wanted.

Jenny Cartier works for First Fiduciary Trust, the bank through which the Dorlands applied for their mortgage. With the Dorlands' permission, Jenny asked for a credit report from Canyon Credit Company. Canyon is one of the three major credit bureaus that First Fiduciary uses.

After an uneventful but anxious three days, the Dorlands received a phone call from Jenny at the bank. She said that the credit report from Canyon showed that the Dorlands had an outstanding lien on a fishing boat in Happy Jack, Louisiana. For that reason, the bank couldn't approve their mortgage application. Arvin was incensed. He told Jenny that there had to be a mistake—that neither he nor Annabelle had ever even visited Louisiana, much less bought a boat there.

Jenny replied that if the Dorlands wanted their dream house and a First Fiduciary mortgage, they'd better get the problem cleared up fast. There was another couple who'd made an offer on the house, and the seller wouldn't wait more than 48 hours. Jenny gave Arvin the name and phone number of Louise Patella, her contact at Canyon Credit.

By law, anyone can get the details of his or her credit report and suggest corrections. Arvin immediately contacted Louise. She researched the problem and discovered another Arvin Dorland, a man from Magnolia, Louisiana. Lousie knew immediately that the company had two different Arvin Dorlands on file—the New Hampshire man was in his mid-thirties; Arvin in Louisiana was 72. Louise promptly corrected the database and issued a new report to First Fiduciary—but not before the Dorlands' dream house had been sold to someone else.

Arvin and Annabelle's concern is that the bank will always associate the Dorlands with "that problem with the boat in Louisiana." Also, they worry that the other two credit companies the bank uses could distribute the erroneous information.

Louise's husband, Peter, also works at Canyon Credit. Peter is the director of systems analysis and design, and he and Louise have often discussed the increasing frequency of complaints concerning incorrect credit reports. After hearing about the Dorlands' problem, he approached the president and chief executive officer of Canyon Credit to suggest a change in the database.

Peter argued that using names to identify a record for retrieval worked fine when the database was small. But now the database system was large and needed to be modified so all records had unique identifiers, or key fields, such as sequential nine-digit numbers. Such a change would allow growth to one billion records and eliminate the mistaken-identity problem.

The president directed Peter to do a full cost-benefit analysis of the matter. Peter discovered that to convert to using numeric identifiers would cost $45,000 and save the company $9,000 per year over the next five years. Peter concluded that, although the analysis did not provide a clear financial reason to proceed with the conversion, the gain in system accuracy would be enough to justify the change. The president, on the other hand, considered the errors in the database a small problem. Based on the long payback period shown by the cost-benefit analysis, he vetoed the change.

CASE WORKSHEET

(See Chapter 3 for details about how to carry out each step of the analysis.)

I. Find the facts
    A. List the relevant facts _____
    _____
    _____
    _____
    _____
    _____
    _____
    _____

    B. List the stakeholders _____
    _____
    _____
    _____
    _____

II. Make a defensible ethical decision
    A. Isolate the ethical issues (Should someone have done or not done something?)
    _____
    _____
    _____

    B. Examine the legal issues _____
    C. Consult guidelines
        Corporate policies, codes of conduct _____
    _____

        Golden Rule _____
    _____

        Who benefits? Who is harmed? _____
    _____
    _____

        Tests for right and wrong _____
    _____
    _____

D. Discover the applicable ethical principles

Least harm _____

_____

Rights and duties _____

_____

Professional responsibilities _____

_____

Self-interest and utilitarianism _____

_____

Consistency and respect _____

_____

E. Make a defensible choice _____

_____

III. Describe steps to resolve the current situation

A. Options _____

_____

B. Recommendation _____

_____

_____

C. Defense _____

_____

D. Implementation _____

_____

E. Short-term corrective measures _____

_____

IV. Prepare policies and strategies to prevent recurrence

A. Describe the organizational, political, legal, technological, or societal changes needed _____

_____

_____

B. Describe the consequences of your suggested changes _____

_____

_____

Something for Everyone
Recombination of Data at a Supermarket

The place: Elm Street, Happy Valley, Massachusetts. Mary Smith returns from the mailbox, sorting the day's arrivals. Her husband, John, is trimming the hedge.

"John, look! We got a coupon in the mail! It's a $15 discount to have Rover groomed. How did they know?"

"Know what?"

"Well, how did Molly's Pet Grooming Service know we have a dog? Do you suppose one of our neighbors told them about Rover?"

"Mary, I can't see how that's likely. It must be one of those hit-or-miss mass mailings. Anyway, let's use that coupon. It sure is a good deal."

Chambord's Supermarket Store #1, Griffin, Massachusetts: Nola Brickell, information systems administrator for the 12-store Chambord chain, talks with her boss, General Manager Pierre Nadeau.

"Pierre, do you remember Molly Graubert, that sweet old woman who asked us if we could sell her a list of pet owners?"

"Yeah? So what does she want now?" Pierre remembers how easy it was to get that list. All customers who pay by check use Chambord's ID cards, which cross-index to their addresses. The check-out scanners log the customers' purchases, duplicating the sales receipts, with details on everything they buy. The receipts include the ID number. All Nola had to do to create the list Molly wanted was to ask the computer for the names and addresses of all people who bought pet food or pet supplies. True, that list didn't include the buyers who paid with cash, but it met Molly's needs.

"Well, I've had three different calls from people who found out about us selling Molly that list. The head of marketing at Relaxed Retirement, the mail-order outfit that sells the Florida condos, wants a list of the people who buy old-age health stuff—you know, denture cream, corn plasters, and such."

"Yeah, so? Who else called?"

"Mr. Campbell, the head of sales at Farwell Ford, asked for a list of the customers who bought maps, vacation-planning guides, and motor oil. I guess he's looking for people who might be in the market for a new car. And here's a strange one: The Sears Appliance Center's floor manager wanted a list of our customers who didn't buy any frozen foods for two weeks in a row. He figured that they wouldn't have a freezer. I told them all no way, of course. But I thought you should know."

Mr. Nadeau is visibly angry.

"Geez, Nola, you can't do that! Do you realize how much money there is in those lists? And it's free money, too. I mean, you can create those lists with no trouble at all, right? Am I right?" He's almost shouting.

"Yes, but . . . It's not right."

"Not right? What do you mean, not right?"

"Well, it's not . . . It just doesn't seem right."

"Geez, Nola, get off it. Our profit margin's around 1 percent. We feel good making a dime on a bag of groceries, and you're telling me it's not right to improve our profit picture? Do you realize that those lists can make us enough money to really compete, to increase our advertising, to have more loss-leaders, to—here's something you probably didn't think about—to increase salaries, including yours? And what can be more right than helping these other salespeople sharpen their marketing lists? And what about our customers? They get a few more flyers in their mailboxes, maybe letting them know about a deal on something they want and need. And don't forget Molly Graubert. We sold her a list, and everybody was happy about that. She doubled her business, and no complaints."

But the names we sell . . . Those people—they don't . . . they didn't . . . "

"They didn't what? Didn't volunteer their names? Don't know about focus marketing? Come on, give them credit for something. Everybody sells lists, you know. Why do you think you get so much mail asking for donations to this and that charity? Because you gave once, that's why, and those people sold their list of donors to all the other charities. Geez, Nola, if charities can do it, why shouldn't private enterprise?"

"Yes, but . . . "

"No buts about it, Nola. Now call those guys back and tell them we'll do it, or it's your job. I mean it. You made a mistake, and you've got to correct it."

Main Street, Hopdale, Massachusetts: Dick and Jane Jones relax in front of the TV, watching a travelogue. It's all about Florida and its wonderful climate for retirees.

Dick turns to Jane and says, "Now, that's my idea of retirement. We've talked about Florida. Do you think we should take a vacation there this year, to check it out for our retirement? It's only a couple of years away."

Jane is thrilled that he mentioned Florida. Why, just today in the mail she got a grand brochure on buying a Florida condominium. "Maybe we should try it out first, on a vacation, like you say. And maybe we should look into buying some housing while we're down there. We could look up those condos that Relaxed Retirement is advertising."

"Yeah. We sure can do better than staying here. You know, it's lucky we didn't get robbed like the Roberts next door, and those nine other working couples last week. In the middle of the day, too. Lucky you don't work. Why, it's almost as if those goons had a list of old folks who have jobs to go to."

CASE WORKSHEET

(See Chapter 3 for details about how to carry out each step of the analysis.)

I. Find the facts
    A. List the relevant facts _____

    _____

    _____

    _____

    _____

    _____

    _____

    _____

    B. List the stakeholders _____

    _____

    _____

    _____

    _____

II. Make a defensible ethical decision
    A. Isolate the ethical issues (Should someone have done or not done something?)

    _____

    _____

    _____

    B. Examine the legal issues _____
    C. Consult guidelines
        Corporate policies, codes of conduct _____

    _____

        Golden Rule _____

    _____

        Who benefits? Who is harmed? _____

    _____

        Tests for right and wrong _____

    _____

    _____

D. Discover the applicable ethical principles

Least harm _____

_____

Rights and duties _____

_____

Professional responsibilities _____

_____

Self-interest and utilitarianism _____

_____

Consistency and respect _____

_____

E. Make a defensible choice _____

_____

III. Describe steps to resolve the current situation

A. Options _____

_____

B. Recommendation _____

_____

_____

C. Defense _____

_____

D. Implementation _____

_____

E. Short-term corrective measures _____

_____

IV. Prepare policies and strategies to prevent recurrence

A. Describe the organizational, political, legal, technological, or societal changes needed _____

_____

_____

B. Describe the consequences of your suggested changes _____

_____

_____

Abort, Retry, Ignore
Recovery of Data Leads to Discovery of Confidential File

It was only 9:10 A.M. and Barry Larson panicked. He was close to hyperventilating. His fingers darted over the keyboard again and again, repeating the DOS command. He kept hoping the system would just once be able to read the disk. "Just once," he thought, "and I'll back it up. Then I can print the report." But the luminous green message kept repeating

Directory error reading drive C: Abort, Retry, Ignore?

Barry was scheduled to attend the regular two-hour staff meeting in 20 minutes. And at 1:30 he was due to submit his quarterly projection report to William Burton, the comptroller of Cardamom Corporation. Barry was out of time. He snatched the phone from the cradle and dialed Technical Support. Barbara Dalton was at his desk in 5 minutes, with her all-time favorite file-recovery tool, Fixit.

"Did you try to write anything to the disk after you saw the message?"

"No! All I've done is try to get into my spreadsheet system!" Barry was almost shouting.

Barbara tried to reassure him. "No sweat, then. I should be able to recover all your files by the time you get back from your morning meeting."

Barry was visibly relieved. He told Barbara, "The only file that's important to me is the worksheet called PROJ3Q. Recover that one and the spreadsheet program, and I'll treat you to lunch for a week."

Barry rushed off to his meeting and Barbara got to work. She started up Fixit in the floppy drive and identified drive C, the hard drive, as the corrupted target. Fixit's first listing showed many file names with a question mark for a prefix, including ?OMMAND, ?RINT, ?ORMAT. She also saw ?ROJ3Q. When DOS erases a file, it only marks the file as "erased" by replacing the first character of the file name with a special character. Fixit simply displays that special character as a question mark. Barbara knew immediately what Barry had done. He had intended to erase the files from a diskette in his floppy drive; instead, by accident, he had addressed his C drive and erased the files there.

"This should be a snap," she thought. "?OMMAND is COMMAND, ?RINT is PRINT . . ."

She started the repairs. System files were easy, as were the spreadsheet files, which all ended with the extension .WKS. She also saw ?ROJ3Q and immediately changed that to PROJ3Q. In 10 minutes she had done all that Barry had asked for. However, Barbara felt that she should rescue more files and guarantee Barry's promise of free lunches. She continued her cleanup of the disk.

The other data files—worksheets and word processing text files—were harder. Barry had made up the names of these files according to some association scheme tied to the contents of the file. First Barbara renamed the files starting with question marks; she made each question mark X instead. ?OSB became XOSB and ?TOCREP changed to XTOCREP. At this point, Barbara could have left the system for Barry to rename all files as he intended.

Barbara, though, was a perfectionist. She had been at the PC for only 20 minutes and had recovered the contents of the hard disk. She knew that the disk directory still needed touching up, however. Barry would have to rename all X-prefixed files to their original names. Barbara knew that Barry would be pressed for time, so she decided to help him out. She was pretty sure that a glance at a file's contents would be sufficient to figure out the file name. She brought up the word processor and started scanning the files, renaming them as she went. XOSB was a memo to the Bank of South Boston, so she changed the file name to BOSB. XTOCREP was a stock report. It was changed to STOCREP.

After cleaning up the text files, Barbara got into the spreadsheet system to look at those files. The first one, XALPAY, came as a complete surprise. It was a listing of Cardamom's salaried personnel, including their current annual salary. She thought, "Barry does a great job as a financial analyst for Mr. Burton, but what in the world is he doing with payroll information?"

She immediately renamed the file SALPAY, trying hard not to look at the contents. Then she continued through the rest of the files, scanning content just enough to rename the files appropriately. After verifying that there were no more files with the X or ? prefix on the disk, she tested the system. It worked well, and she felt confident that Barry could reclaim and print his precious quarterly projection file. On his desk she left a note listing all the files she had renamed.

CASE WORKSHEET

(See Chapter 3 for details about how to carry out each step of the analysis.)

I. Find the facts

    A. List the relevant facts _____

_____

_____

_____

_____

_____

_____

_____

    B. List the stakeholders _____

_____

_____

_____

_____

II. Make a defensible ethical decision

    A. Isolate the ethical issues (Should someone have done or not done something?)

_____

_____

_____

    B. Examine the legal issues _____

    C. Consult guidelines

        Corporate policies, codes of conduct _____

_____

        Golden Rule _____

_____

_____

        Who benefits? Who is harmed? _____

_____

_____

        Tests for right and wrong _____

_____

_____

D. Discover the applicable ethical principles

Least harm _____

_____

Rights and duties _____

_____

Professional responsibilities _____

_____

Self-interest and utilitarianism _____

_____

Consistency and respect _____

_____

E. Make a defensible choice _____

_____

III. Describe steps to resolve the current situation

A. Options _____

_____

B. Recommendation _____

_____

_____

C. Defense _____

_____

D. Implementation _____

_____

E. Short-term corrective measures _____

_____

IV. Prepare policies and strategies to prevent recurrence

A. Describe the organizational, political, legal, technological, or societal changes needed _____

_____

_____

B. Describe the consequences of your suggested changes _____

_____

_____

Messages from All Over
Who Controls the Content of E-Mail and BBS?

The HMV Corporation is one of the largest designers and manufacturers of distributed computer systems. Its phenomenal growth in the last decade is due in large measure to its attention to networking technology. It makes extensive use of its own product, operating one of the largest computer networks in the world. Most of HMV's 107,000 employees have access to the network, and they are encouraged to use it. The two most popular network services that HMV employees enjoy are their own bulletin board system, or BBS, and electronic mail, or e-mail.

The BBS is intended to serve exactly as the name implies, as a sort of computer-managed announcement board. The company encourages its employees to swap technical information openly and quickly. A user interested in new developments in supercooled switches would only have to enter a few descriptive words, such as "cryogenic & switching time & superconductive" to get all messages relating to the topic. HMV's policy allows the BBS users to treat the board as a kind of classified-ads network. Although the majority of messages are of the "Notice" variety, an increasing number of "Wanted" and "For Sale" items appear. An employee interested in selling a house to a fellow HMV worker might enter, for example, "for sale & house & Chicago."

The e-mail system is intended as the private communications medium for the company. The user may send messages to one or to many receivers. Messages to groups of users, such as those in regional offices or specific research labs, are about as common as messages from one individual to another. Of course, if someone wanted to send a message to all HMV employees, that user would use the BBS.

Horace Ganglion is the network administrator. His responsibilities, aside from keeping the system running at all times, include on-line monitoring of BBS message content. He must keep the BBS from becoming too cluttered with items that would more properly belong in a newspaper. Also, he must ensure appropriate use of the e-mail system.

Bill is Horace's assistant network administrator. He has asked to see Horace on a matter of some urgency. Bill's responsibilities include acting as liaison between network users and Horace. Bill shows Horace a hard-copy listing of messages. Bill selected them while he was scanning the traffic out of curiosity. Horace sees that this list is a photocopied compilation of output created by using the PRINTSCREEN key.

These messages were all on the BBS:

Notice: Some PC clones (Shrinq, Dill, Howland-Parker, others) bomb when moving data from one open file to another when using MegaWrite. For more info contact . . .
Voters: Send Washington a message! Dump Bush and vote for Duke!
For Sale: Indonesian love slave. Grants your every wish. Contact . . .
Notice: Are there any real sports out there ready for a fun indoor game? Contact . . .
Wanted: Decent word processor, manuals unnecessary, no questions asked. Contact . . .

Horace read the list of e-mail messages that Bill had selected:

To:. . . , VP Mktg
From: . . . , Phoenix Training Center Stock Manager
Date: . . .
Subject: Available Hardware
Our office has several used PC clones available for internal sale at a very reasonable price. Those not sold internally will be greatly discounted on the open market. Send me a message if you're interested.
To: . . . , Manager, Systems Development Group
From: . . .
Date: . . .
Subject: Dorothy Vinson
Among many other comments I have received concerning Dorothy's work performance are the following: "Incapable of approaching business negotiations in a professional, rational, and mature manner . . . ," " . . . shouldn't be trusted . . . ," "her actions were intended to alarm, manipulate, antagonize, or further disrupt the process . . . "
What do you suggest I do now?
To: . . .
From: . . .
Date: . . .
Subject: Private consultation
Are you interested in some indoor sport?
To: . . .
From: . . .
Date: . . .
Subject: Termination
One more leak about that Garfinkel deal behind my back, and you're gone, buster! I'm the boss around here, and if I say Garfinkel is clean and knows what he's doing, then that's the way it is. I don't care what kind of dirt you might have dug up on him—he stays our contractor. And the fact that he's my cousin has nothing to do with it. Got it?

Horace knows that he has to do something about some of the senders of these messages. Although the company has a flexible policy on message content, his job includes the monitoring of the system to prevent its misuse.

What does Horace do?

CASE WORKSHEET

(See Chapter 3 for details about how to carry out each step of the analysis.)

I. Find the facts
    A. List the relevant facts _____
        _____
        _____
        _____
        _____
        _____
        _____
        _____
        _____

    B. List the stakeholders _____
        _____
        _____
        _____
        _____

II. Make a defensible ethical decision
    A. Isolate the ethical issues (Should someone have done or not done something?)
        _____
        _____
        _____

    B. Examine the legal issues _____
    C. Consult guidelines
        Corporate policies, codes of conduct _____
        _____

        Golden Rule _____
        _____
        _____

        Who benefits? Who is harmed? _____
        _____
        _____

        Tests for right and wrong _____
        _____
        _____

D. Discover the applicable ethical principles

Least harm _____

_____

Rights and duties _____

_____

Professional responsibilities _____

_____

Self-interest and utilitarianism _____

_____

Consistency and respect _____

_____

E. Make a defensible choice _____

_____

III. Describe steps to resolve the current situation

A. Options _____

_____

B. Recommendation _____

_____

_____

C. Defense _____

D. Implementation _____

_____

E. Short-term corrective measures _____

_____

IV. Prepare policies and strategies to prevent recurrence

A. Describe the organizational, political, legal, technological, or societal changes needed _____

_____

_____

B. Describe the consequences of your suggested changes _____

_____

_____

CASE 6

A Job on the Side
A Consultant Is Tempted to Moonlight

Mitron is a billion-dollar computer hardware and software vendor. Anthony Frasier is a software-support analyst for Mitron's Midwest field office. Anthony is on the phone with customers much of the time. He reports the customers' program bugs to Engineering, and he gives his customers software patches or workarounds directly over the phone lines, computer-to-computer, whenever possible.

When Anthony hears about difficult software problems, he takes his expertise to the customer personally. Until last year, his on-site support and occasional user training were provided as a part of the customers' maintenance contracts. That practice became so popular that it was too expensive for Mitron. They had to change the policy of free support and training, so they unbundled the support services from the maintenance contract. Now Mitron charges its customers separately for on-site support services.

Mitron suffered during the past recession. Management's response to the crunch was to freeze all salaries for 18 months. Twelve months have passed, and Mitron still hurts. Some people have been laid off, and Anthony suspects that his days are numbered. However, he knows he is still valuable to Mitron; his supervisor told him that he'd be the first to get a raise, if that were possible.

One of Mitron's largest customers and one of Anthony's most important clients is the state government. Over the years, he has established a close relationship with many key state employees. The state has several sites where employees need a lot of technical help and training; the users prefer to contract with Mitron rather than to develop the expertise from within. Anthony has been working closely with Mary Coulter in the State Information Systems Office. They know each other well and have developed an enviable level of mutual trust.

Yesterday, Mary called Anthony.

"Anthony, I have a proposition for you to think about."

"Shoot."

"State needs someone at the Pastoria site to help out with their new system. It's the new PAX 3355 system your people installed this summer, and they need support and training in the worst way. It's right up your alley. Want to do it?"

"Sure. Send up the paperwork and I'll get started."

"Wait, you don't understand. I want *you* to do this, not Mitron. If we get you through the company, it'll take months of paperwork. And we have to pay the Mitron overhead fees, besides."

"Gee, I don't know, Mary. You're asking me to do something on my own that my company pays me for. Isn't that a conflict of interest?"

"Well, that depends. Your company's present policy on that really should change, don't you think? Like when they unbundled service from maintenance. Anyhow, we want you rather than some other consultant we don't know, even if they're cheaper. You know, success at this site in Pastoria means a lot of future business to Mitron. My feeling is that they'd go along with this if we explained it to your management."

"Why don't you? What's the rush? Why don't you present your case to our management? Maybe they can hurry up the process, get you an answer in a couple of weeks."

"Anthony, you don't understand. We can't wait that long. And the sooner the system is up and running, the better it will be for the entire state. Don't forget that one of the big reasons we got this system was to reduce the delay of payment on welfare and unemployment compensation. We won't ask you for any time that would interfere with your normal work schedule. You name the hours, show up when you can, and we know you'll do the job. To make it worth your while, we'll pay you 20 percent above the usual consulting fee, and give you a $5,000 bonus when you're through."

Anthony said nothing. He is pleased that his reputation is so good. He is overwhelmed at the generosity of the offer. He considers it to be the chance to start up a decent nest egg in case he's laid off. He wonders at the consequences if word gets out ...

CASE WORKSHEET

(See Chapter 3 for details about how to carry out each step of the analysis.)

I. Find the facts
    A. List the relevant facts _____
        _____
        _____
        _____
        _____
        _____
        _____
        _____

    B. List the stakeholders _____
        _____
        _____
        _____
        _____

II. Make a defensible ethical decision
    A. Isolate the ethical issues (Should someone have done or not done something?)
        _____
        _____
        _____

    B. Examine the legal issues _____
    C. Consult guidelines
        Corporate policies, codes of conduct _____
        _____

        Golden Rule _____
        _____
        _____

        Who benefits? Who is harmed? _____
        _____
        _____

        Tests for right and wrong _____
        _____
        _____

D. Discover the applicable ethical principles

Least harm _____

_____

Rights and duties _____

_____

Professional responsibilities _____

_____

Self-interest and utilitarianism _____

_____

Consistency and respect _____

_____

E. Make a defensible choice _____

_____

III. Describe steps to resolve the current situation

A. Options _____

_____

B. Recommendation _____

_____

_____

C. Defense _____

_____

D. Implementation _____

_____

E. Short-term corrective measures _____

_____

IV. Prepare policies and strategies to prevent recurrence

A. Describe the organizational, political, legal, technological, or societal changes needed _____

_____

_____

B. Describe the consequences of your suggested changes _____

_____

_____

CASE 7

The New Job

An Offensive Start-up Screen
Appears in an Office Environment

Iris is really upset, and she seems to have no one to go to. Two weeks ago, she was brimming with excitement about her new job. Now, she wonders whether she should quit.

Tolliver Investments is a rising star in the highly competitive field of brokerage houses. It's only three years old, and it has grown from a trio of entrepreneurs with a few loyal friends as its customers to a company with 37 employees and lots of hustle. Tolliver has succeeded in a tight economy where many others have failed, in large measure because of the 15 brokers that make up the Customer Service Group.

Iris Blair has been with Tolliver Investments for two weeks. In her newly created job of applications manager, Iris installs, maintains, and upgrades all the company's software tools, from word processors, spreadsheet programs, and utilities, to graphics and statistical packages. She and Terry Sullivan, the customer services manager, report directly to Roy Tolliver, the president and CEO. Iris knows that her performance for the next several weeks will be the deciding factor in her career.

Tolliver's Customer Services Group is the backbone of the company. The brokers have available to them all the modern technology possible in each of their offices, which they call their bullpens. Each bullpen has a 12-line phone system and three high-resolution color graphics computers, each one capable of accessing, as a terminal, any stock market worldwide. The computers can also act as independent workstations to perform financial analyses, word processing, or any other stand-alone activity.

Terry Sullivan's idea of management is that it's best to have the brokers in the bullpens slightly out of control and free to think for themselves, so his grip on them is loose, almost detached. Terry knows that those 15 people are the company's breadwinners and that each earns about as much on commission as Roy Tolliver does. They could leave anytime, so they have to be kept happy.

Terry has networked the 45 computers to a 12-gigabyte disk drive that acts as a central server. The brokers call this drive Mother. At each desk, the workers also have 88-megabyte removable-cartridge disk drives. Terry encourages his brokers to use the cartridges for temporary storage and for their individual operating systems. He wants to keep Mother for the various versions of the software Tolliver uses. His policy has resulted in all brokers having individualized machines, each with its own start-up screen and its customized "signature" system software.

Two nights ago, after most people had left, Iris was in the office of Arthur Amanita and Ronald Conway, two of the most highly respected brokers at Tolliver. Her job was to install a new virus-protection program. She noticed that Art and Ron's 88-meg system cartridges were in their protective cases, properly shelved away from the hardware. Art and Ron were gone for the day. She inserted Art's cartridge and booted the system. The screen lit and, instead of the usual smiling-face start-up screen, the display showed a bikini-clad woman in a provocative pose. After about 15 seconds the screen blinked, then showed the usual desktop. Iris installed the virus-protection software, shut down Art's computer, and repeated the process on one of Ron's computers. The start-up screen was exactly the same as Art's.

Yesterday morning, Iris was in early, as usual. When she saw Art and Ron go past her office, she approached them and told them that she had installed the virus-protection software last night. They stopped with Iris at her desk.
Art said, "So, what do you think of our high-resolution start-up screens?"
Iris replied, "Why don't you guys grow up? That's so sophomoric."
Art's smile disappeared. He faced Iris and said nothing, his eyes burning into hers. Then he grinned. "Iris, you need to loosen up. Tell you what. How about you and me stopping by Googol's Bar after work. Then I'll treat you to dinner, and who knows what after?"
"Thanks, but no. I expect I'll still be here tonight when you're long gone."
"Fine by me," Art said. But obviously it was not.

At noon today, Iris passed by Art's office. Art wasn't in, but Ron was in his next-door bullpen. He called her to his desk.
"Wait a sec. You want to see our latest start-up screen? It's a major improvement."
He rebooted his machine, and this time the start-up screen showed a woman in full-frontal nudity.
Iris fumed. "Now, that's really tasteless and insensitive. You should know better." She heard Ron's reply behind her as she stomped out of the office.
"Hey, it's your fault. Maybe you shouldn't have refused Art's invitation."

Iris sees Roy Tolliver and Art laughing together at the coffee counter. She knows it's about the start-up screen. She catches Tolliver glancing in her direction and lowering his voice. They laugh again, this time more quietly. It's obvious to Iris that these two are doing their male bonding at her expense. "That's just great," she thinks. "Now there's no telling what I might find the next time I boot a system. Is this job worth it?"

CASE WORKSHEET

(See Chapter 3 for details about how to carry out each step of the analysis.)

I. Find the facts
    A. List the relevant facts _____

        _____

        _____

        _____

        _____

        _____

        _____

        _____

    B. List the stakeholders _____

        _____

        _____

        _____

        _____

II. Make a defensible ethical decision
    A. Isolate the ethical issues (Should someone have done or not done something?)

        _____

        _____

        _____

    B. Examine the legal issues _____
    C. Consult guidelines
        Corporate policies, codes of conduct _____

        _____

        Golden Rule _____

        _____

        Who benefits? Who is harmed? _____

        _____

        Tests for right and wrong _____

        _____

        _____

D. Discover the applicable ethical principles

Least harm _____

_____

Rights and duties _____

_____

Professional responsibilities _____

_____

Self-interest and utilitarianism _____

_____

Consistency and respect _____

_____

E. Make a defensible choice _____

_____

III. Describe steps to resolve the current situation

A. Options _____

_____

B. Recommendation _____

_____

_____

C. Defense _____

_____

D. Implementation _____

_____

E. Short-term corrective measures _____

_____

IV. Prepare policies and strategies to prevent recurrence

A. Describe the organizational, political, legal, technological, or societal changes needed _____

_____

_____

B. Describe the consequences of your suggested changes _____

_____

_____

The Buyout
Inappropriately Acquired Data
Prompts Personnel Problems

Agaric Software started small, grew fast, and met its fate in a quick buy-out by Spectran Corporation. At first, Agaric employees assumed they would keep their autonomy and operate with little change in management or method. Such was not to be the case. Spectran wanted a merger so that Agaric would be a branch office, with only a portion of its original staff.

Mary Marver is and has been general manager of Agaric for three years. Her staff respects and admires her for her managerial ability and her loyalty. They call her Marverlous Mary. She knows about the nickname and likes it.

Mary has participated in all negotiations with Spectran, so she is aware of the eventual fate of some of its employees. Filed under the name PROJTEN, she has a Lotus spreadsheet that projects future employment of the staff. It lists present workers, their current projects, their lengths of tenure at Agaric, their current salaries, and their scheduled termination dates. Mary protects this file with an encryption utility called DESCANT. This program uses the Data Encryption Standard (DES) algorithm to jumble any file via a key, or password, supplied by the user. Mary's password is MARVERLOUS.

Louis Shuster's phone rings. "Hi, Lou. Rick. Hey, it looks like we Pattersons will get countrified. Sally and I found the house we want—it's a beaut. Can't wait to tell you about it. How about lunch at noon?"

"Sure. See you in the caf. Bye."

Louis Shuster and Rick Patterson have been with Agaric for years. They are tight and trusting friends. Rick is, at this moment, critical to the company's future success with Spectran. He is managing the transfer of all service accounts from Agaric to Spectran's support staff. His value is due in large measure to his upbeat outlook and friendly attitude with outsiders. Louis's job is entirely different: He deals with Agaric programmers only, and then just to get bugs fixed or to get upgrades to the software he uses.

Unknown to Louis and Rick, they are both included in Spectran's decision to reduce the payroll by 25 percent. Spectran wanted this cut to occur on May 1, with no notice but with a two-week–salary severance package. Mary Marver had argued with Spectran: She said the people must be kept until the transfer of all Agaric customers was complete. Spectran agreed to hold off the cuts until June 1, the deadline for transfer, but not any longer. They also agreed, at Mary's insistence, that all people to be terminated would be given a minimum of one month's notice to reduce their personal hardships. But

Spectran's management insists that Rick is an exception. He must not be told of his impending layoff until the end of the contract, because he must keep a "happy face" during his work with the clients. Spectran's explanation was simple: "Rick Patterson is valuable to us until June 1. After that date, his job will be assumed by people in Spectran. It would be counterproductive to keep him on the payroll for a month if his job is gone."

On May 1, all affected employees, except Rick, are notified of the massive layoff a month away. Louis is one of the notified workers, and he is understandably upset, but only for a few days. He quickly finds another job, and he will start work for his new company in two weeks. Louis is glad that Rick was not one of those given notice.

While still working at Agaric, Louis needs the name of a project proposal. He knows that the names, both tentative and final, are in a file on Mary's hard disk. He must find the name to complete his work, so he looks for Mary to ask her for a copy of the name file. Mary is tied up in meetings, so Louis sits at her desktop computer and boots it. Mary's directory lists a file called PROJTEN, but he sees it's been protected by DESCANT. He assumes the name PROJ-TEN stands for PROJect TENtative.

He has no idea what Mary's password is. He looks around: Nothing taped to her desk or the computer, no strange name penciled onto the desk edge, no family picture with kids' names. He thinks a minute. "What would Marverlous Mary use . . . That's it!"

Louis types MARVERLOUS as a password and gains access to PROJTEN. It's a worksheet. He brings it up onto the screen and sees some names and projects, but one glance tells him that none of the listed projects is tentative. Then he notices the column headings "Tenure at Agaric" and "Termination date." He sees his own name with the date June 1. Rick Patterson is there too, with the same date. But Rick wasn't notified. Has some mistake been made?

Louis restores the computer to its original state and returns to his desk to finish the day. He is reluctant to say anything because he has invaded Mary's private file. The next three days are agony to Louis, but he keeps mum.

On the fourth day after the layoff notice, the phone rings. Louis thinks, "I bet that's Rick. They finally told him."

"Hello, Louis Shuster here."

"Hi, Lou. Rick. Guess what?"

"Yeah, I know. Isn't it awful? I wanted to tell you, but . . . "

"Awful? What do you mean, Lou? It's great! Sally just called. She borrowed on our insurance and made the down payment on that house. Just had to call you to let you know. Looks like my luck is holding. What was that you wanted to tell me?"

"Well, er . . . Rick, we have to talk. Let's meet for lunch. Noon."

CASE WORKSHEET

(See Chapter 3 for details about how to carry out each step of the analysis.)

I. Find the facts
    A. List the relevant facts _____
    _____
    _____
    _____
    _____
    _____
    _____
    _____
    _____

    B. List the stakeholders _____
    _____
    _____
    _____
    _____

II. Make a defensible ethical decision
    A. Isolate the ethical issues (Should someone have done or not done something?)
    _____
    _____
    _____

    B. Examine the legal issues _____
    C. Consult guidelines
        Corporate policies, codes of conduct _____
        _____

        Golden Rule _____
        _____
        _____

        Who benefits? Who is harmed? _____
        _____
        _____

        Tests for right and wrong _____
        _____
        _____

D. Discover the applicable ethical principles
    Least harm _____

    _____

    Rights and duties _____

    _____

    Professional responsibilities _____

    _____

    Self-interest and utilitarianism _____

    _____

    Consistency and respect _____

    _____

E. Make a defensible choice _____

    _____

III. Describe steps to resolve the current situation
    A. Options _____

        _____

    B. Recommendation _____

        _____

        _____

    C. Defense _____

        _____

    D. Implementation _____

        _____

    E. Short-term corrective measures _____

        _____

IV. Prepare policies and strategies to prevent recurrence
    A. Describe the organizational, political, legal, technological, or societal changes needed _____

        _____

        _____

    B. Describe the consequences of your suggested changes _____

        _____

        _____

CASE 9

Charades
A Stolen Password and Its After-Effects

Good morning, class. This week's assignment is simple. See if you can get into the school's mainframe operating system. You've been reading all about password protection and its weaknesses. Now you're to see if you can beat the RACS Network. If you succeed in stealing a network user's password, you are to log in to their account; print a simple document with the user name on top, as usual; and log off. You are not to add, delete, or modify any of the user's files. Otherwise, there are no rules. Anything goes, even social engineering. To the limit, people."

Social engineering is a confidence game that hackers use on unwary timesharing users to steal their passwords. It involves the use of intimidation, pretense, gall, and outright lying.

Dr. Peter Proctor's class, called Computer Security and Privacy, is one of Lagonda College's most popular, due in large part to Dr. Proctor's challenging "TTL" assignments. His students call them TTLs because he generally uses the phrase "to the limit" for emphasis.

Last week, he demonstrated social engineering. He called a fellow faculty member and said, "Sorry to interrupt your busy schedule. This is Karl Oberfest, systems administrator. I need your password to clean your account of borschtic. Afterwards you can change it . . . OK, thanks."

Florence Porter and Ann Galen are two of the top students in the class. They generally plot together to solve the TTLs. This time, though, Florence decides to go it alone. They are sitting side by side at two terminals in the student computer lab.

"Ann, I just can't seem to get logged in. I've tried and tried, but I get bounced off every time. I bet there's something wrong with this terminal."

"Oh, come on! You know better than that. It's got to be something you're doing wrong in your log-in procedure. Try again, only slower."

Florence bashes the keys once more. Again, she turns to Ann.

"I just can't get it. Ann, I know it sounds silly, but just log off and switch terminals with me and *you* try it. Please."

Ann and Florence switch places. Ann sees this on the screen:

```
RACS Network
USER NAME:>
```

Ann enters her user name, "Galen." The screen now shows:

```
USER NAME:>Galen
PASSWORD:
```

Ann looks around. Florence has turned her back, a common courtesy to avoid discovering another's password. Ann enters her password carefully, one character at a time, and receives this message:

```
Access denied on try 1.
Disconnected. Reconnect to try again.
```

Curious, she thinks. She knows she has two more tries after reconnecting. She tries again.

```
RACS Network
USER NAME:>Galen
PASSWORD:>********
Welcome to RACS Operating System
$
```

"Florence! I got in. It was just a fluke."

"Yes, Florence? You got someone's password without their knowledge? Let's see your printout." Dr. Proctor is clearly surprised and pleased. The printout shows Ann Galen's name at the top.

"Ann, were you aware that your password was compromised? You didn't give it to Florence, did you?"

"Of course not! But how did she do it? I'm very careful about that," Florence explained.

"I wrote a program that displays the system's prompts. Then I pretended that I had trouble logging in, remember? We switched terminals and you thought you were logging in. But you were really interacting with my program, not the system. It captured your password and placed it in a file in my account, then gave you the 'Disconnected' message and logged off. When you logged in a second time, you weren't in my account anymore, but in the system. It's called the charade technique. Slick, huh?"

Dr. Proctor reminded the class about the hazards of social engineering and congratulated Florence for a job well done. He further explained the charade technique and several other common methods for stealing passwords.

Professor Whitten has just called roll in the Introduction to Programming Techniques class. A hand in the back is raised and waiving.

"Yes, George?"

"My files on the RACS are gone. I didn't delete them. Did Lagonda change the system around, or what?"

"My files are gone too."

"Mine, too. . . "

"Mine, too. . . "

CASE WORKSHEET

(See Chapter 3 for details about how to carry out each step of the analysis.)

I. Find the facts
   A. List the relevant facts _____
   _____
   _____
   _____
   _____
   _____
   _____
   _____

   B. List the stakeholders _____
   _____
   _____
   _____
   _____

II. Make a defensible ethical decision
   A. Isolate the ethical issues (Should someone have done or not done something?)
   _____
   _____
   _____

   B. Examine the legal issues _____
   C. Consult guidelines
   Corporate policies, codes of conduct _____
   _____

   Golden Rule _____
   _____

   Who benefits? Who is harmed? _____
   _____

   Tests for right and wrong _____
   _____
   _____

D. Discover the applicable ethical principles
Least harm _____

_____

Rights and duties _____

_____

Professional responsibilities _____

_____

Self-interest and utilitarianism _____

_____

Consistency and respect _____

_____

E. Make a defensible choice _____

_____

III. Describe steps to resolve the current situation
A. Options _____

_____

B. Recommendation _____

_____

_____

C. Defense _____

_____

D. Implementation _____

_____

E. Short-term corrective measures _____

_____

IV. Prepare policies and strategies to prevent recurrence
A. Describe the organizational, political, legal, technological, or societal changes needed _____

_____

_____

B. Describe the consequences of your suggested changes _____

_____

_____

Laccaria and Eagle
Restrictive Trade Practices Call
for Hard Purchasing Decisions

Laccaria is a large South American country located between Brazil and Argentina. Its new military government understands the strategic importance of a strong information technology industry. Government officials feel that, to encourage technological growth, they must impose strict protectionist measures. These will help ensure that emerging Laccarian firms will be able to take full advantage of the domestic market, the ninth largest in the world. The trade barriers and high tariffs are not imposed on larger-scale computers, arbitrarily classified as mainframes by Laccarian officials.

The imposition of these protectionist measures has resulted in the formation of many small and medium-sized high-tech firms. They either assemble components imported from abroad or they manufacture Laccarian clones of equipment made by large U.S.A. vendors such as Epsilon. In many cases, the locally produced equipment is copied exactly from U.S. equipment—often without licensing agreements.

Laccaria has many software houses to support this manufacturing effort. Although the government of Laccaria has international copyright agreements with the United States, Laccarian officials often look the other way, allowing local software houses to make and market unauthorized copies of U.S. software.

Multinational corporations that operate branches or subsidiaries in Laccaria have felt the effect of the protectionist measures. It is difficult to get the right hardware configurations to run the software specifically designed for use at overseas sites. Sometimes a planned system cannot be implemented because some critical part, such as a multiplexer, is not available in Laccaria.

Eagle Bank is a large holding company headquartered in the United States. It has a network of international offices in nearly 40 countries. At most of these international sites, Eagle Bank has installed Epsilon System 45s from Epsilon Corporation of Syracuse, New York. The hardware uses Eagle's Corporate Core Software Package. However, all seven of the Eagle-Laccaria sites are operating in batch mode with punched cards and tape drives. The systems haven't been upgraded because the Laccarian government's Informatics Bureau lists the System 45 as a minicomputer, so it cannot be imported from the United States or neighboring countries.

The manager of Eagle-Laccaria's head office asked Carlo, his DP manager, to contact Orista, the Laccarian vendor that makes a system similar to the System 45. The Laccarian system is called the Orista 45K. Carlo discovered that using these clones would force major changes to the Corporate Core Software Package, and that the hardware price was $270,000—almost three times the price of the same configuration in the United States. Carlo also found that the Orista 45K hardware was unreliable and subject to frequent breakdowns, that Orista lacked what he called "a properly trained maintenance staff," and that the firm offered poor support.

Carlo's next step was to talk to his contact at the Informatics Bureau. When Carlo asked what could be done, his bureau contact suggested that Eagle-Laccaria purchase an Epsilon mainframe, the 4311, a machine manufactured by Epsilon in Laccaria. Unfortunately, it costs $380,000—$30,000 higher than its U.S. price.

During the discussion, Colonel Cuervo of the Informatics Bureau warned Carlo not to get into difficulty by purchasing a "parallel market" System 45. These are Epsilon System 45s that have been brought into the country illegally. These may look tempting, he said, because they cost only $120,000 and are made in the United States. However, these "unofficial import channels" are not recognized by the government, which considers them detrimental to the economy of Laccaria. Carlo knows, though, that many firms in Laccaria, some competing directly with Eagle, have these illegal machines. The government rarely prosecutes violators of its protectionist policy.

The manager must make his decision. Carlo has supplied him with this simple summary table:

MACHINE	SOURCE	COST	NOTES
Orista 45K	Orista	$270,000	Unreliable Poor service Software changes necessary Good for local economy, in the government's opinion
Epsilon 4311	Epsilon-Laccaria	$380,000	Too much machine Software conversions needed
Epsilon 45	Parallel market	$120,000	No changes to software Known entity Bad for local economy, in the government's opinion

The manager studies the table and tells Carlo, "It's obvious, isn't it?"
Is it?

CASE WORKSHEET

(See Chapter 3 for details about how to carry out each step of the analysis.)

I. Find the facts
    A. List the relevant facts _____

        _____

        _____

        _____

        _____

        _____

        _____

        _____

    B. List the stakeholders _____

        _____

        _____

        _____

        _____

II. Make a defensible ethical decision
    A. Isolate the ethical issues (Should someone have done or not done something?)

        _____

        _____

        _____

    B. Examine the legal issues _____
    C. Consult guidelines
        Corporate policies, codes of conduct _____

        _____

        Golden Rule _____

        _____

        _____

        Who benefits? Who is harmed? _____

        _____

        _____

        Tests for right and wrong _____

        _____

        _____

D. Discover the applicable ethical principles

Least harm _____

_____

Rights and duties _____

_____

Professional responsibilities _____

_____

Self-interest and utilitarianism _____

_____

Consistency and respect _____

_____

E. Make a defensible choice _____

_____

III. Describe steps to resolve the current situation

A. Options _____

_____

B. Recommendation _____

_____

_____

C. Defense _____

_____

D. Implementation _____

_____

E. Short-term corrective measures _____

_____

IV. Prepare policies and strategies to prevent recurrence

A. Describe the organizational, political, legal, technological, or societal changes needed _____

_____

_____

B. Describe the consequences of your suggested changes _____

_____

_____

Taking Bad with Good
The Software Is Bad, So Don't Pay for It

Aldrich & Thayer (A&T) is a multimillion-dollar financial services company. The firm uses old batch-oriented programs for its daily operations. Each day A&T used its old programs, it became less competitive. It was desperate to replace the batch system with an up-to-date networked system of applications. The Information Systems Department had targeted two batch programs for immediate replacement. One performed stock-and-bond analysis, and the other managed client transactions.

MegaMerge Software is the developer of MoneyMaker, a financial-analysis applications package sold to small investment firms. Among its several subprograms, two were of special interest to the Information Systems Department of A&T. FINSTAT performs analyses on stocks and bonds, and CLIENTS manages buyer transactions. MegaMerge has never tried Money-Maker at any site larger than Murdock's, the local investment company, which has a multiuser microcomputer with eight terminals in separate offices. Murdock's was considered to be MegaMerge's beta test site. That is, MegaMerge gave Murdock's the package of applications free of charge, with the understanding that Murdock's would report any bugs to MegaMerge.

A number of key people from A&T's Information Systems (IS) Department observed MoneyMaker in operation at Murdock's and saw that it was an excellent tool. They liked FINSTAT especially. The department decided to convert to network status. A&T purchased MoneyMaker, aware that it would have to customize the programs to suit its own unique needs. The contract specified that A&T purchase MoneyMaker for $10,000 payable upon delivery, plus $800 a month for maintenance and upgrades.

The company invested time and money to assemble a conversion team. This so-called Project X Team was a group of 14 new employees, some permanent and some contract workers. The Project X Team's objective was to change MoneyMaker from a client system for a small, single-site investment office to one that would work in a network environment.

A&T knew that MoneyMaker had not been fully tested, so it included these points in its contract with MegaMerge:

- Buyer (Aldrich & Thayer) is aware of the "raw" nature of the product.

- Seller (MegaMerge) will supply buyer with four new releases per year to add new functionality to the system and to correct minimal bugs.

- Seller makes no guarantee of safety or accuracy of the package.

- Seller is responsible for "functional generic package errors." If such errors occur, Seller will fix them and give Buyer the code or create a new release.

The contract did *not* include:

- A standard for testing the software.

- The amount of testing Seller would do before the package was released.

- A disclaimer clause proclaiming Seller not responsible for Buyer's lost profits or damage to Buyer's reputation due to problems with software.

From the first day of testing by Project X programmers, it became evident that MoneyMaker had both very good and very bad features. The stock-and-bond analysis program, FINSTAT, was far better than anything A&T had used in the past—even better than MegaMerge's sales representative had said it was. Also in FINSTAT's favor, it worked beautifully in A&T's networked environment, equally well at all sites.

Unfortunately, the other MoneyMaker program, CLIENTS, which A&T wanted to use to replace its client management program, was a total disaster. It worked fine in a small environment, but no amount of rewriting could make it operate efficiently and accurately in a large network.

A&T had spent much time and money in its efforts to customize Money-Maker, but it couldn't make use of any of MoneyMaker's programs except FINSTAT. Besides the conversion costs, A&T had paid MegaMerge $6,400 for maintenance for eight months. The firm had received quarterly upgrades from MegaMerge, but none helped the problems with CLIENT. The IS Department's manager estimated that, without CLIENT in operation, 50 percent of MoneyMaker's functionality was gone.

After consulting with the IS Department manager, the chief financial officer of A&T decided to reduce the maintenance and upgrade fee of $800 to $400 a month in compensation for the lost value of CLIENT.

When MegaMerge's manager heard of this reduction in payments and the reasons for it, he had his best programmer write a virus program to destroy all MegaMerge programs at A&T. The virus was placed in the next upgrade shipment to A&T. When A&T installed that upgrade, the virus destroyed all MegaMerge programs, including FINSTAT, which had become A&T's workhorse program.

A&T stopped all payment to MegaMerge and sued the firm for malicious destruction of property. MegaMerge countersued A&T for nonpayment for contracted services.

CASE WORKSHEET

(See Chapter 3 for details about how to carry out each step of the analysis.)

I. Find the facts
    A. List the relevant facts _____
        _____
        _____
        _____
        _____
        _____
        _____

    B. List the stakeholders _____
        _____
        _____
        _____
        _____

II. Make a defensible ethical decision
    A. Isolate the ethical issues (Should someone have done or not done something?)
        _____
        _____
        _____

    B. Examine the legal issues _____
    C. Consult guidelines
        Corporate policies, codes of conduct _____
        _____

        Golden Rule _____
        _____

        Who benefits? Who is harmed? _____
        _____

        Tests for right and wrong _____
        _____
        _____

D. Discover the applicable ethical principles

Least harm _____

_____

Rights and duties _____

_____

Professional responsibilities _____

_____

Self-interest and utilitarianism _____

_____

Consistency and respect _____

_____

E. Make a defensible choice _____

_____

III. Describe steps to resolve the current situation

A. Options _____

_____

B. Recommendation _____

_____

_____

C. Defense _____

_____

D. Implementation _____

_____

E. Short-term corrective measures _____

_____

IV. Prepare policies and strategies to prevent recurrence

A. Describe the organizational, political, legal, technological, or societal changes needed _____

_____

_____

B. Describe the consequences of your suggested changes _____

_____

_____

CASE 12

The Engineer and the Teacher
Copyright Ethics in Schools and Industry

My name is Harrison Granger. Three months ago, I was hired as senior engineer by Googalong Consultants in Dallas. The firm's clients are local utility companies that need solutions to civil, structural, mechanical, and electrical problems. I manage these projects and deal with the associated clients.

The competition for winning consulting contracts is fierce. When my company started in business two year ago, it had only a few personal computers and the bare minimum of engineering, accounting, and office automation software.

As the company grew, it added more PCs and circulated more copies of the original software, along with unauthorized versions of more sophisticated software tools. There were no funds to buy legitimate software. In fact, the company canceled maintenance contracts on the hardware and operating system software during these lean times.

Now, we're located in a new office park. Business is booming in a slumping economy, because the company focus is on quality work at a reasonable price.

Just yesterday my boss told me that he wanted me to take over as manager of Information Systems Resources. It's not that big a deal. It takes only one day a week to keep track of all the software we have, making sure we have backups of the most recent versions and so on.

What bothers me is what I found on this job during the first day. The company's bread-and-butter software, the engineering package we use all the time, the one that is the envy of all our competition, was never purchased. It is a bootlegged copy.

Well, of course I went to my boss.

He said, "My gosh! You don't expect us to buy that now, do you? It costs $10,000 in bare-bones form. Spending that kind of money would set us back years against the competition. I expect we'll be able to afford it in a year or two, but right now we wouldn't be able to make competitive bids if we were to buy it."

My name is Esther Gooch. Three months ago, I was employed as an adult education teacher for a consortium of several San Francisco–area schools.

This group of schools has set a goal for me and the other AE teachers: We must teach relevant skills and technologies to the area's adult population. Unfortunately, the recent budget cuts undertaken in California towns and cities have forced the teaching staff to stretch all existing resources. We are asked to teach computing without having adequate software.

When I first began three months ago, I was told by my fellow teachers that the only way we could make an impact would be to teach the skills that sell, such as word processing and spreadsheet development, and to use the most current and popular software. Of course, I agreed. But I pointed out that site licenses for these products are expensive. I told them that single-copy versions of decent, though less popular, software packages are often available free, as freeware.

My fellow teachers thought, however, that we have a moral right—and maybe even an obligation—to make multiple copies of "good" software to distribute to as many educators as might find it useful. Even the administrators turn their heads at the practice. They feel the same way the teachers do: Without copied software, the students would not learn the leading-edge software and would stop coming to our classes. Ultimately, we'd be out of a job.

I have a hard time swallowing the line that the software developers are losing money on potential sales. There's no way we could buy it. Besides, by exposing our students to the software, we're training a large pool of potential future customers.

I think it's my moral duty as an educator to give my students the best possible training with the most up-to-date tools. I'm not alone in this opinion, either. Many civic groups donate software and hardware to these schools. They know the good job we're doing, and they know we couldn't do a proper job without some degree of software copying.

What bothers me, though, is this: What are we teaching our students about the value of copyrights when they know they're using bootlegged copies, and they know we know it?

CASE WORKSHEET

(See Chapter 3 for details about how to carry out each step of the analysis.)

I. Find the facts
    A. List the relevant facts _____
        _____
        _____
        _____
        _____
        _____
        _____
        _____

    B. List the stakeholders _____
        _____
        _____
        _____
        _____

II. Make a defensible ethical decision
    A. Isolate the ethical issues (Should someone have done or not done something?)
        _____
        _____
        _____

    B. Examine the legal issues _____
    C. Consult guidelines
        Corporate policies, codes of conduct _____
        _____

        Golden Rule _____
        _____
        _____

        Who benefits? Who is harmed? _____
        _____
        _____

        Tests for right and wrong _____
        _____
        _____

D. Discover the applicable ethical principles

Least harm _____

_____

Rights and duties _____

_____

Professional responsibilities _____

_____

Self-interest and utilitarianism _____

_____

Consistency and respect _____

_____

E. Make a defensible choice _____

_____

III. Describe steps to resolve the current situation

A. Options _____

_____

B. Recommendation _____

_____

_____

C. Defense _____

_____

D. Implementation _____

_____

E. Short-term corrective measures _____

_____

IV. Prepare policies and strategies to prevent recurrence

A. Describe the organizational, political, legal, technological, or societal changes needed _____

_____

_____

B. Describe the consequences of your suggested changes _____

_____

_____

Test Data
Confidential or Dummy Data?

The Connecticut Cautionary Insurance Corporation (CCIC) is a multibillion-dollar life insurance company with over three million policyholders. J. William Willow heads CCIC's corporate Data Systems Development (DSD) Group. The DSD Group is responsible for producing and maintaining all programs that manage CCIC's insurance policies. Sybil Bonham heads a team of three programmers who work in DSD as systems analysts. Their responsibilities include the analysis and design of many programs, and often their coding and maintenance.

Sybil, the lead analyst on the development of the insurance-policy service program, was recruited last year by Bill Willow to help the DSD Group improve the reliability of their software products. Sybil's leadership prompted the DSD Group to adopt several improved software engineering practices such as walkthroughs, top-down development, and structured techniques. She also recommended the automated test-data generation tools that the DSD Group now uses routinely. The insurance-policy service program was the first software product developed using these tools and techniques.

Two weeks ago, the Whole Life Annuity Analysis program bombed on its first run on real data, and it took several hours to locate and fix the bug. Sybil went to the archive database to find the flaw that caused the program's failure. The error documentation file in the archive database showed that the instruction to calculate average annual gain divided the sum of interest by the policyholder's age in years. The real data had a case where the age of the policyholder was zero years.

Sybil explained to Bill Willow that her program had been tested to meet all user specifications, but how could she be sure that the user specifications provided the rules to account for all valid data? She concluded that she could uncover some of the specification flaws by testing her program on live data from the Policyholder file. Bill became adamant, indicating that customer data is confidential information and is available only for production runs. Sybil explained that specification errors could not be generated with the test-data software, that she could uncover these types of errors only by running her program against live data. Bill refused to allow this breach of the company's rules.

Sybil became angry. "Bill, you and I both know that if we had tested this program with live data from the Policyholder file, we'd have discovered that specification error and probably many others besides. And we both know that the group couldn't care less what the data represents. It can't be a breach of confidentiality if we don't look at the data, can it? Please, let us use live data and get this job done right."

Bill responded with equal force. "No. It's company policy, and I'm not going to let you compromise it. Run the program on test data. If another specification error stops it, we'll correct that and repeat the process until we get it right."

One hour ago, the revised program ran for a third time against artificial test data, and failed again on yet another specification error. Sybil again pleaded with Bill to allow a test on live data. After all, the group had run the program on test data twice already, expecting flawless performance. But in both cases, the program crashed, forcing yet more changes.

Bill has a problem. His boss, the vice president for Information Systems, has been pressuring him to get the group to release the Whole Life Annuity Analysis program. He's irritated with Sybil for her constant pleas to use live data, and he feels stymied by the company policy. Somehow, he's got to get the project moving again. He is sorely tempted to use Sybil's suggestion. He knows that if he does, he can get this program into production within the week.

Bill calls Sybil into his office to discuss the program and its future testing. He says, "OK, here's what we do . . . "

CASE WORKSHEET

(See Chapter 3 for details about how to carry out each step of the analysis.)

I. Find the facts
    A. List the relevant facts _____
        _____
        _____
        _____
        _____
        _____
        _____
        _____

    B. List the stakeholders _____
        _____
        _____
        _____
        _____

II. Make a defensible ethical decision
    A. Isolate the ethical issues (Should someone have done or not done something?)
        _____
        _____
        _____

    B. Examine the legal issues _____
    C. Consult guidelines
        Corporate policies, codes of conduct _____
        _____

        Golden Rule _____
        _____
        _____

        Who benefits? Who is harmed? _____
        _____
        _____

        Tests for right and wrong _____
        _____
        _____

D. Discover the applicable ethical principles

Least harm _____

_____

Rights and duties _____

_____

Professional responsibilities _____

_____

Self-interest and utilitarianism _____

_____

Consistency and respect _____

_____

E. Make a defensible choice _____

_____

III. Describe steps to resolve the current situation

A. Options _____

_____

B. Recommendation _____

_____

_____

C. Defense _____

_____

D. Implementation _____

_____

E. Short-term corrective measures _____

_____

IV. Prepare policies and strategies to prevent recurrence

A. Describe the organizational, political, legal, technological, or societal changes needed _____

_____

_____

B. Describe the consequences of your suggested changes _____

_____

_____

The Brain Pick
A Knowledge-Based System Can't Know Everything

The Davis Stamp Company of Bismark, North Dakota, is the second-largest company in the world that caters to the needs of philatelists, or stamp collectors. It sells stamps, albums, catalogues, and every kind of accessory any collector could want. It has a reputation for fairly pricing its rare stamps, taking into consideration their condition and authenticating them as genuine when there is any doubt. Alex MacPhearson and Joan Andrews are two experts at Davis who are often called upon to judge the value and authenticity of especially rare stamps.

The Scan-Do Corporation of Phoenix, Arizona, announced its Model 720 high-resolution flatbed color scanner last year. It won rave reviews from every critic. It is easy to use, can differentiate over 16 million shades, and has a resolution of 600 dots per inch. Although its cost exceeds $17,000, it is unique in the marketplace. Unfortunately, it hasn't been a big seller, in part because no one has developed a need for its high-quality features. Monica Burke's job is to change that. She is a consultant, a knowledge engineer whose assignment is to develop the software for the expert system called PhilaTeller, an automated postage-stamp evaluator.

Monica is in Bismark to meet with Alex and Joan of Davis Stamp and to work with them for two months. She is there to develop a computerized questionnaire that Alex and Joan, and any other philatelic expert, can answer to build the knowledge base for PhilaTeller. PhilaTeller is now in its so-called infancy, containing as a database the entire contents of *Weston's United States Specialized Stamp Catalogue*. If PhilaTeller works for the high-priced U.S. stamps, Scan-Do experts think it can work for all other countries' stamps and for other stamp companies.

Because Moncia is a stamp collector as well as a knowledge engineer, she feels confident that she can produce the questionnaire in less than the allowed time. For three weeks, Monica asks about dimensions and printing; perforation; color transfer; types; and gross and fine errors, from cracked plates to missing frame lines. Her questionnaire is developing nicely, but she begins to sense a reticence on the part of Alex and Joan. They occasionally seem vague in their answers.

"What can I ask about the paper? Thickness? Color? Kind?"

Joan hesitates, then says, "I'm not sure I can word a question for you on that. Sometimes the paper just feels right, and sometimes I know it's wrong. It's not thickness, or transparency, or color, or anything like that. It's almost like . . . a feeling, something I just know. Like knowing that a strange dog likes you. You don't know why, but something tells you it won't hurt you."

"What about you, Alex? Can you be more specific so that we can put it into question form?"

"Unfortunately, I agree with Joan. Oh, sure, some details are easy to measure, like thickness and color. But I seem to sense some qualities that I can only attribute to experience. For example, I can't tell exactly why I can differentiate parchment types from rag paper or thick paper types. I guess that's why Joan and I get big bucks for our judgments."

Monica frowns. She makes a few more attempts to get more information, then moves on to the next area. She feels that she can fill in the gaps herself.

Two years later, several large companies and dealers use PhilaTeller as a trusted tool in judging incoming stamps from collections. One day the following news story appears:

Dallas Register (IP) — Computer Fails to Spot Rare Stamp. Hortense Gneiss of Hopewell, Texas, is suing the Bondurance Stamp and Coin Company for $1,000,000 for failure to perform professionally and misrepresentation of expertise. Gneiss alleges that an expert system called PhilaTeller did not correctly identify a Danish West Indies stamp she sold to Bondurance in a collection. Although Gneiss did not know it at the time of the sale, the stamp was what collectors call a Three Palms Blue on Parchment. The stamp is supposedly worth in excess of $750,000.

The collection, which she sold to Bondurance for $120,000, was later sold to the Davis Stamp Company of Bismark, North Dakota. The Three Palms Blue was discovered by Alex MacPhearson, who was working as a private consultant for the Davis Company. MacPhearson was helping to divide the collection into small job lots for easier sale.

The expert system, which is a program designed to act like an expert when fed the right questions, was developed by Scan-Do Corporation of Phoenix, Arizona. Representatives of Scan-Do could not be reached for comment.

CASE WORKSHEET

(See Chapter 3 for details about how to carry out each step of the analysis.)

I. Find the facts
    A. List the relevant facts _____
    _____
    _____
    _____
    _____
    _____
    _____
    _____
    _____

    B. List the stakeholders _____
    _____
    _____
    _____
    _____

II. Make a defensible ethical decision
    A. Isolate the ethical issues (Should someone have done or not done something?)
    _____
    _____
    _____

    B. Examine the legal issues _____
    C. Consult guidelines
    Corporate policies, codes of conduct _____
    _____

    Golden Rule _____
    _____
    _____

    Who benefits? Who is harmed? _____
    _____
    _____

    Tests for right and wrong _____
    _____
    _____

D. Discover the applicable ethical principles

Least harm _____

_____

Rights and duties _____

_____

Professional responsibilities _____

_____

Self-interest and utilitarianism _____

_____

Consistency and respect _____

_____

E. Make a defensible choice _____

_____

III. Describe steps to resolve the current situation

A. Options _____

_____

B. Recommendation _____

_____

_____

C. Defense _____

_____

D. Implementation _____

_____

E. Short-term corrective measures _____

_____

IV. Prepare policies and strategies to prevent recurrence

A. Describe the organizational, political, legal, technological, or societal changes needed _____

_____

_____

B. Describe the consequences of your suggested changes _____

_____

_____

Trouble in Sardonia
Do Copyright Ethics Change Overseas?

Luke Atwater is on the fast track at JKL Corporation, headquartered in Dallas, Texas. JKL is a billion-dollar firm specializing in heavy-duty oil-well drilling and pumping equipment. Luke's last job was to manage the start-up of a marketing branch in Chicago; there, among other tasks, he was responsible for installing all hardware and software for the branch office. The office was really the entire 15th floor, 23 rooms in all, of the Sears Tower. He had to network PCs for all offices with the appropriate productivity software. This included spreadsheet systems, word processing software, and the JKL Corporate Marketing Package.

Luke completed the job in only four months, even though Pamela Courant, his immediate supervisor, had given him six months to do it. Pamela is the corporate vice president for Information Systems, in Dallas.

Now Luke is in his next posting, in Russula, Sardonia, trying to repeat his stunning Chicago performance. He's been here for four months already, and practically nothing has happened except that the old Wisteria Hotel has been remodeled into some semblance of an office building. He knows he's got to pick up the pace or his job will be up for grabs.

As Pamela told him over the phone before he left: "Luke, I expect more from you now. The Sardonia office is our third international office, but it could be the key to all of Europe. It has to be in the black—that means profitable, making us money—in six months. I'll give you those six months as I did in Chicago, but I expect you to do better than that."

Luke remembers his misgivings at meeting this newest deadline. Sardonia's pace is definitely slower than Chicago's, due to its easygoing culture and stultifying bureaucracy. But he sees one unexpected compensation for the difficulties he has encountered: Sardonia's economy is far less developed than it could be. Anything JKL does for this country will be greatly appreciated and will reflect well on the company.

Luke expects no problems with the hardware. JKL managed the trans-shipment of all PCs from its headquarters in Dallas. All Luke had to do was to notify Pamela exactly what he needed: how many PCs of what type, how big a central server, and how many feet of cable. The shipment came in yesterday, and the parts are already being distributed. Luke knows that there will be some of the usual problems with wiring, but resolving them shouldn't take more than a week or two.

The real problem, Luke thinks to himself, is going to be the commercial software for word processing and spreadsheeting. Pamela specifically requires that all JKL offices use Multisoft's MultiGrid and MultiWrite. Luke has been in phone contact with Multisoft for the past two days. He described the layout of the office, including the number of stand-alone PCs and those that would use a central server. In Chicago, the cost for site licenses for such a setup would be $1,500 for 10 to 19 users and $2,500 for 20 to 49 users. He was surprised to learn that—for international sites, including Sardonia—the costs are $3,500 and $5,500, respectively.

Luke calls in his software manager, Grifolo Frondoso, a native Sardonian familiar with both packages.

"Grif, I want you to order MultiGrid and MultiWrite for our office. How many copies of each do you think you'll need?"

"Well, I should get at least 35 of each, if you expect this office to grow during the next year. We've got enough money budgeted for that. It shouldn't add up to more than about $200 U.S."

"I hate to give you the bad news, Grif, but Multisoft wants $5,500 for that many users. That's way beyond our $1,000 expense limit."

"That makes no sense, boss. We don't have to order from Multisoft here. I can get you copies of the software for a buck over the cost of the diskettes, all legal and aboveboard."

"Sure, but that's not the latest release. Besides, that's copyrighted software. You can't do that."

"Yes, we can, here in Sardonia. The U.S. software copyright laws don't apply here. We can get as many copies as we want of the newest versions. Or, we could order one fresh copy from Multisoft and make copies."

"Even if we decide to do that, we'd be without manuals. We've got to have manuals at each station, so that kills your idea. And don't forget future revisions . . . "

"No problem. We can copy the manuals, too, or we can pay a local printer who needs the work to print high-quality copies for about $3 each. That still falls under the $1,000 limit, by a long shot. And don't worry about revisions. We'll get them, too."

Luke stands up and walks to the window overlooking Russula's oppressive slums, saying nothing. He's deep in thought for some time, then turns to Grifolo Frondoso.

"Here's my decision. We'll . . . "

CASE WORKSHEET

(See Chapter 3 for details about how to carry out each step of the analysis.)

I. Find the facts
    A. List the relevant facts _____
        _____
        _____
        _____
        _____
        _____
        _____
        _____

    B. List the stakeholders _____
        _____
        _____
        _____
        _____

II. Make a defensible ethical decision
    A. Isolate the ethical issues (Should someone have done or not done something?)
        _____
        _____
        _____

    B. Examine the legal issues _____
    C. Consult guidelines
        Corporate policies, codes of conduct _____
        _____

        Golden Rule _____
        _____
        _____

        Who benefits? Who is harmed? _____
        _____
        _____

        Tests for right and wrong _____
        _____
        _____

D. Discover the applicable ethical principles

Least harm _____

_____

Rights and duties _____

_____

Professional responsibilities _____

_____

Self-interest and utilitarianism _____

_____

Consistency and respect _____

_____

E. Make a defensible choice _____

_____

III. Describe steps to resolve the current situation

A. Options _____

_____

B. Recommendation _____

_____

_____

C. Defense _____

_____

D. Implementation _____

_____

E. Short-term corrective measures _____

_____

IV. Prepare policies and strategies to prevent recurrence

A. Describe the organizational, political, legal, technological, or societal changes needed _____

_____

_____

B. Describe the consequences of your suggested changes _____

_____

_____

Downtime
Overdependence on Computers Means Trouble

Rod Wantage has a full-time job as a programmer-analyst at JPT Corporation. JPT Corporation supplies product distributors with inventory management systems. These systems all work with a large database accessed through a multiuser microcomputer with up to 50 terminals. The name of the system, TrackPiece, is the same, whether the distributor using it sells auto parts, pet supplies, or novelty items. Only the databases change.

The usual cost for TrackPiece is $8,000 for the software, plus $750 per month for online services, including backup, maintenance, and troubleshooting. Included in that $750 per month is what JPT calls its Feel Well Plan, a hot-site backup facility at their headquarters that automatically takes over the inventory operations of any client whose hardware crashes. A client's contract for JPT's TrackPiece explicitly states that to supply this backup, JPT must have continuous on-line access to any client database. It's this feature that allows JPT to guarantee uptime for any user. This feature also causes some people to complain about the system's reaction time: Because of the heavy traffic to and from JPT's home site, it takes about a minute for the client's database to be updated.

On his own time, Rod is a computer consultant to small businesses. His business card reads:

Rodney Wantage
Software Engineer, Consultant
President and CEO
RW COMPUTER SERVICES

He works out of his home, writing most of his own software. In some cases he reverse-engineers commercial packages to suit the needs of his small-business clients. Rod is in Spandril's Auto Repair, a three-bay garage owned and operated by Stan Spandrill.

"Say, Stan, you got that '73 Fairlane taillight assembly I ordered?"

"Sure, Rod. Just a minute. I'll get it for you."

Stan is back shortly with a box in hand. "You're in luck. My distributor had it, so he didn't have to back order. Fact is, he hardly ever does, with that new TrackPiece inventory system of his. It's too bad JPT doesn't make a cheaper version of that software for us small-time garages. We could keep track of what we have, and we could make sure we don't stock what we don't need."

Rod looks around Stan's small office and notes that there aren't any waiting customers. "You know, Stan, if you have a minute or two, I'll explain my programs to you. They'll let you do just what your distributor does with his JPT stuff, except cheaper. Also, you know the big complaint about Track-Piece—that one-minute delay between the time you place an order and when your database gets corrected? Well, my system cuts that down to less than a second!"

"Yeah? What about manuals? You know, we've never used one of those programs in here. We've got a lot to learn."

"Don't worry. My system is completely menu-driven. And it uses color coding, so using it is easy. I don't have to supply manuals, because the program's so simple. Besides, I'll be a phone call away in case of trouble."

Six months later, Rod's TrakPart system is installed at Stan Spandril's garage. The first few weeks were hectic as Rod constantly debugged the system of its spate of flaws. However, once the inventory figures were transferred to the TrakPart database, Stan's confidence in the system increased significantly. He is so confident in his new system, in fact, that he has not bothered to keep any manual data on hand. He got rid of all of his manually maintained counts because he trusts the computer's tallies. Why, just last week the computer told him he had 14 AQX halogen headlamps. When he went back to the shelf to check, out of curiosity, he counted only 12. Sure enough, when he got back to the front desk Clyde Mungo, the new trainee, was entering the sale of two AQX halogen headlamps.

This morning, quite by accident, Clyde entered the wrong part number while processing the sale of 12 fan belts. When the system asked for a correction, Clyde didn't know how to do it, so he tried to cancel the entry by entering a sale of –12 fan belts and using the same invalid part number. The system balked, coughed, spat, and died. Clyde went to Stan, who called Rod.

It is 5:30 P.M. and Rod has just arrived. He wanted to come earlier, but he was in the midst of a file conversion at JPT and couldn't get away. Now he is trying to unravel the errors without destroying the database in the process. Stan is ready to kill Rod, or at least maim him, for his "highfalutin promises of a fast system!" Even if he can find the parts, he's now afraid to sell them for fear of getting the inventory out of balance. All day, he's been turning customers away.

"I'd like a radiator hose, please, for my '88 Caddy."

"Sorry, George. Not until that computer comes up."

"Hi, Stan. Could you get me two 15-amp fuses, please? For my pickup."

"Sorry. Not until that darn computer comes up."

"How about one of those custom floor mats?"

"Sorry, Wendy. Not until the computer comes up."

CASE WORKSHEET

(See Chapter 3 for details about how to carry out each step of the analysis.)

I. Find the facts
    A. List the relevant facts _____
        _____
        _____
        _____
        _____
        _____
        _____
        _____

    B. List the stakeholders _____
        _____
        _____
        _____
        _____

II. Make a defensible ethical decision
    A. Isolate the ethical issues (Should someone have done or not done something?)
        _____
        _____
        _____

    B. Examine the legal issues _____
    C. Consult guidelines
        Corporate policies, codes of conduct _____
        _____

        Golden Rule _____
        _____
        _____

        Who benefits? Who is harmed? _____
        _____
        _____

        Tests for right and wrong _____
        _____
        _____

D. Discover the applicable ethical principles

Least harm _____

_____

Rights and duties _____

_____

Professional responsibilities _____

_____

Self-interest and utilitarianism _____

_____

Consistency and respect _____

_____

E. Make a defensible choice _____

_____

III. Describe steps to resolve the current situation
A. Options _____

_____

B. Recommendation _____

_____

_____

C. Defense _____

_____

D. Implementation _____

_____

E. Short-term corrective measures _____

_____

IV. Prepare policies and strategies to prevent recurrence
A. Describe the organizational, political, legal, technological, or societal changes needed _____

_____

_____

B. Describe the consequences of your suggested changes _____

_____

_____

CASE 17

Code Blue
Patient Data at a Hospital Is Compromised

Metropolitan General Hospital is a large urban institution known for the efficient management of resources. The Information Systems Department at MGH has been transitioning from a centralized to a distributed system. Presently, MGH uses its mainframe for most administrative, research, and patient-information databases. Access to this powerful system is through smart terminals and PCs acting as terminals. The PCs also act as stand-alone word processors and file managers at most sites throughout the hospital.

There are PCs at each nurses' station on each of the hospital's 20 floors. Each PC has software that can access the main system and download that station's present patient information. The nurses can interact with the PC to access patient data, thus reducing both response time and the load on the mainframe.

One of the busiest areas is on the third floor, West Wing. This is the Vehicular Accidents area. Only the most serious accident victims are brought to this ward; the simple concussions, lacerations, and broken limbs end up elsewhere. Here, every case is touch-and-go, requiring much attention and vigilance.

On her computer screen, Nurse Betty Blodgett has just brought up the record of Nathaniel Barker, the patient in room 15. She has a copy of the accident report at her desk and is reading the medical record page by page from the local file server. She discovers that Barker—age 37, 6 feet 3 inches tall, 170 pounds, and with a red beard—was riding his Harley Davidson at dusk heading east. He was about to start a gentle left turn when an approaching westbound Mercedes station wagon lost the curve in the setting sun. The head-on collision conformed to Newton's laws exactly. It slowed the big German car perceptibly, and it reversed the Harley's direction in 0.23 milliseconds.

Nurse Blodgett is absorbed in the scrolling medical report. After reading a page, she taps the space bar, both to advance to the next page and to let the software know she's active at the keyboard. The Information Systems Department has purposely designed all software that displays patient information to blank the screen and quit the job if the user doesn't interact in 60 seconds.

Suddenly the intercom blares "Code Blue, room 23. Code Blue, room 23!"

Betty reacts immediately. She leaves at a run to get the crash cart and assist in room 23. She leaves the station unstaffed, but that's standard in an emergency.

Melody Burns is a candystriper volunteer who desperately wants to be a nurse. She has been helping out in the ward for a month now, comforting the patients in their agony, distributing ice water, boofing pillows, and doing the simple tasks that so greatly help the nurses. She gets off the elevator to an empty station. But she heard the Code Blue call, so she knows where they all are. She sees the PC screen fully lit, with a patient's record still on it.

"Ah, Mr. Barker! He's so nice. Of course he can't talk, with his jaw wired and bandaged, but his eyes tell so much. Let's see what his record says. He weighs 170 pounds? Gee, I'd have guessed less, he's so thin. Appendix operation. Blood type A positive. HIV positive. What? HIV positive? My gosh, I had no idea . . ." The screen blanks, and Melody walks out of the nurses' station just as Nurse Blodgett returns.

"Melody! So glad to see you. We sure have had a busy afternoon. Mr. Barker's got his jaw working again, and he's asked to see you the minute you come in. He's so appreciative, as we all are, of the great work you've done . . . Why, Mel, what's the matter?"

"I just can't see Mr. Barker anymore. I'm sorry. It's just that, well . . . maybe I've been spending too much time with him at the expense of the other patients. And besides, I can't get too close to him. I might get AIDS."

Betty is shocked. "What do you mean? What makes you think something like that?"

CASE WORKSHEET

(See Chapter 3 for details about how to carry out each step of the analysis.)

I. Find the facts
    A. List the relevant facts _____
        _____
        _____
        _____
        _____
        _____
        _____
        _____

    B. List the stakeholders _____
        _____
        _____
        _____
        _____

II. Make a defensible ethical decision
    A. Isolate the ethical issues (Should someone have done or not done something?)
        _____
        _____
        _____

    B. Examine the legal issues _____
    C. Consult guidelines
        Corporate policies, codes of conduct _____
        _____

        Golden Rule _____
        _____
        _____

        Who benefits? Who is harmed? _____
        _____
        _____

        Tests for right and wrong _____
        _____
        _____

D. Discover the applicable ethical principles

Least harm _____

_____

Rights and duties _____

_____

Professional responsibilities _____

_____

Self-interest and utilitarianism _____

_____

Consistency and respect _____

_____

E. Make a defensible choice _____

_____

III. Describe steps to resolve the current situation

A. Options _____

_____

B. Recommendation _____

_____

_____

C. Defense _____

_____

D. Implementation _____

_____

E. Short-term corrective measures _____

_____

IV. Prepare policies and strategies to prevent recurrence

A. Describe the organizational, political, legal, technological, or societal changes needed _____

_____

_____

B. Describe the consequences of your suggested changes _____

_____

_____

Virtual Success

Virtual-Reality Games Invade the Real World

Planet Studios, like the major studios competing with Disney and Universal, is a conglomerate made up of many companies that supply the entertainment industry with everything from silver for film to people as contract actors. It includes theater chains, movie and TV hardware, entertainment parks, and even a high-technology research center. Planet's FX Group, located on a 3,500-acre ranch outside Santa Monica, started out 10 years ago as a small lab with 12 engineers. Now, with 285 employees, it is a major manufacturer of high-technology entertainment hardware, such as arcade games and home entertainment accessories.

The latest product to come out of FX Group is a series of virtual-reality, or VR, arcade games. Much R&D effort went into this product, and it seems to be paying off. The two games FX has released for sale are GTP, a simulation of a high-performance race car at the Limerock Rack Track in Connecticut, and Real Flight, which simulates the takeoff, flight, and landing of a Piper Cherokee from Meigs Field in Chicago. Both games supply all the sensory data—sight, sound, G forces, even the smell of fuel and burning rubber. The price of these game machines is high, but demand for them is encouraging.

FX is successful, but trapped in a financial squeeze of its own creation. To get its leading-edge position in the marketplace, the designers of the VR games were always encouraged to use the best hardware to make the sensory cues seem as real as possible. The present models use four RISC processors, but the competition still uses microprocessors of a more traditional design. The added processors make the FX product functionally superior, but greatly reduce the profit margin. FX is looking for a "cash cow," a highly profitable product or a major long-term contract that will allow the group to balance the budget and provide future growth.

Julia Parker is president and chief executive officer of FX. She has called a meeting with Michael LaPlante, VP of future projects, and Jim Wall, lead programmer and technical wizard in the Future Projects Department. The three are to meet with Ted MacDonald, who is chief of technical support for the FBI training facility in Quantico, Virginia. None of the three FX people know exactly what Mr. MacDonald will propose, but they chat informally in the board room with high hopes that maybe he represents the break they've been looking for, a government contract. Mr. MacDonald is ushered in, and, after a round of introductions and ubiquitous coffee, he presents his proposal.

"The FBI needs versions of your arcade games, but modified so that they can be used in realistic training situations rather than for entertainment. We want ... " Ted MacDonald used overhead transparencies to list the FBI's needs:

- A variant of Real Flight, but with a helicopter, in different settings (such as city and country, day and night).

- A variant of GTP, except using an armored personnel carrier in counter-terrorist settings. This product will train agents to use machine guns, and 40-millimeter cannon and accustom them to being shot at.

- A new product to provide small-arms training against realistic foes who mix with innocent civilians. This product will be more realistic than current products for the same purpose and so will help save lives.

After discussing many questions, Mr. MacDonald leaves for Quantico. He expects FX's decision within the week.

The meeting in the board room is now much more uninhibited. Jim Wall says, "It can be done, and easily. Both GTP and Real Flight are based on the same internal hardware. It makes no difference to the hardware whether we're landing an airplane or shooting someone. It will take some intense programming, but that's what they'll pay us the big bucks for, right?"

Michael LaPlante's enthusiasm is less evident. "I'm worried about the FBI's third proposal. I just don't like the idea of training people to kill, even if it's in their line of duty. I could go along with the other two projects, though, as long as we concentrate on the look and feel of the settings and don't get into 'taking out targets,' as the man said in his presentation."

Julia Parker must make the final decision. She must weigh the assured success of the company if it takes on the FBI proposal against a risky, possibly doomed future if FX continues on its present course.

CASE WORKSHEET

(See Chapter 3 for details about how to carry out each step of the analysis.)

I. Find the facts
   A. List the relevant facts _____

   _____

   _____

   _____

   _____

   _____

   _____

   _____

   B. List the stakeholders _____

   _____

   _____

   _____

   _____

II. Make a defensible ethical decision
   A. Isolate the ethical issues (Should someone have done or not done something?)

   _____

   _____

   _____

   B. Examine the legal issues _____
   C. Consult guidelines
       Corporate policies, codes of conduct _____

   _____

       Golden Rule _____

   _____

   _____

       Who benefits? Who is harmed? _____

   _____

   _____

       Tests for right and wrong _____

   _____

   _____

D. Discover the applicable ethical principles

Least harm _____

_____

Rights and duties _____

_____

Professional responsibilities _____

_____

Self-interest and utilitarianism _____

_____

Consistency and respect _____

_____

E. Make a defensible choice _____

_____

III. Describe steps to resolve the current situation

A. Options _____

_____

B. Recommendation _____

_____

_____

C. Defense _____

_____

D. Implementation _____

_____

E. Short-term corrective measures _____

_____

IV. Prepare policies and strategies to prevent recurrence

A. Describe the organizational, political, legal, technological, or societal changes needed _____

_____

_____

B. Describe the consequences of your suggested changes _____

_____

_____

INDEX